DO YOU HEAR MY VOICE?

Do You Hear My Voice?

Discovering Jessica Again

BRUCE KLEIN

Geminae LLC

Copyright

Contents

Foreword

To the Reader

It is an immense privilege to welcome you to this work, which has special meaning to me. I feel blessed to have played some small part in the events described on the following pages, but more so to bear witness of the impact they have had on the author, as well as those within his spiritual circles.

It has been such a delight to get to know Bruce, both as a friend and now as a fellow leader within the local spiritual community. I was fortunate enough to be introduced to him through a dear friend who also happened to be his co-worker. Shelli referred Bruce to me for a spiritual reading in hopes of helping him make sense of his catalyst experience with the voice known as 'Jessica.' He booked me, probably reluctantly, but also in need of understanding of what was happening to him and why.

As a spiritual mentor, medium, and channel, I often get referral clients that are just awakening spiritually. Bruce had been having his experiences for a while, but he was the first client I encountered who asked specifically about "twin flames." I have been offering clairvoyant readings for more than twenty years to a diverse group of clients, yet I didn't have any substantive knowledge or insights about the subject which I could offer him. Although I had heard of twin flames (or twin souls), I held nothing more than familiarity with the term.

The term, twin flame, implies that twin flames or twin souls hold a particular heart and are somehow more deeply intertwined than soulmates. Lifetime after lifetime, many of us make contracts with the same group of souls to help each other learn important lessons about relationships and love. Those are our soulmates, but now I understand that the dynamic between twin flames or twin souls is profoundly different than soulmates.

Although Bruce inquired about twin flames before his reading, he had not yet divulged his experiences with Jessica. Yet, during the reading, images of the divine masculine and feminine came through clearly...specifically the Hindu god, Lord Shiva, and his beloved wife, Parvati. I shared with Bruce that it was clear to me his spiritual work was meant to center around the themes of the divine masculine and feminine and how important the balance and interplay between the two are. Before he left that day, I felt compelled to gift him with a selenite tower that had split into two nearly identical pieces. Selenite is a crystallized, semi-transparent form of gypsum that has been considered most sacred throughout history. The name 'Selenite' derives from the Greek goddess Selene, the goddess of the moon. Jessica was definitely working through me that day to make sure Bruce would soon understand the depth of their connection. She also wanted to gift him with a lovely representation of that connection: two parts that form one whole.

Sometime after the reading, Bruce enlightened me to his amazing experiences, which became just the beginning of the beautiful love story he has so expertly shared on the following pages.

Disclaimer: If you are unsure or not yet a believer in reincarnation, Bruce's experiences may offer you some powerful insights that are guaranteed to broaden your views on the subject. Although I already possessed an unwavering belief in reincarnation, Bruce's accounts of his interactions with Jessica continually deepen my understanding of the enduring nature of love, the importance of connection, and the intelligence and resilience of the human heart.

A few months after Bruce generously shared the details of his journey, he approached me for a regression hypnosis session to explore the depth of his interactions with Jessica. As you will see in the chapters ahead, the session added some beautiful and intimate details about the nature and importance of their relationship. It also offered clarity and a level of tenderness beyond what either of us could have imagined. Jessica's most recent life experience reminded me so much of my mother's that I knew without a doubt the motives, purpose, and gifts from that life were now her personal gift of understanding and compassion to me.

We cannot have such profound spiritual experiences and not be changed in some way. I have been blessed to witness Bruce's transformation. His experiences have informed how he shows up in his friendships and how he has stepped into his gifts. He has dived head-first into mediumship, for which he is especially gifted. He is a clairvoyant and a channel who took to the work as a fish takes to water, and through it, he has become a trusted and beloved leader and a teacher for those around him. Although often perplexed by his journey, he has also fearlessly embraced it. This includes the influences and tribulations around his religious upbringing, which he transmuted into a healing experience for himself and others by creating the podcast "When Religion Unravels." Each episode features a guest who has gone through the bitter and scathing trial of losing their religion only to eventually find their true Self, sometimes even forging a new, more loving relationship with the Divine. Bruce leads and guides these guests with a strong sense of purpose and a gentle but unmistakable integrity.

I am so grateful that Bruce listened well to the unique voice he heard that fateful day. Through his personal story, he affirms for us again and again that love never dies. It does, however, get more creative at making the new-millennia version of a mixtape! And, as Jessica proves through her wisdom (and earworms), there is no better soundtrack than the voice of the one who knows you and loves you beyond time, space, and dimensions.

As you read this amazing love story, may your heart find the sacred, precious, and infinite rhythm of your own "Jessica."

Much love,

Jacki Campbell
Lynnwood, WA

Preface

For many of you reading this book, it may be difficult to accept and believe some of the things I wrote here. Keep in mind, I am a skeptic at heart, and if you had presented much of the contents to me, even a few years earlier, I would have laughed and mocked the very things that I have been through as being fantasies. I would like to ask that when you read this, you suspend your disbelief for just the time that you are reading and ask, "What if?"

What if the contents of this book are true? What if love does go beyond this life? What if there are a host of beings that are on the other side of the veil just waiting to assist us in ways that we can only imagine? If this is true, does that change your perception of the world?

Introduction

Lao Tzu wrote in *Tao Te Ching*, "When the student is ready, the teacher will appear." It took me a long time and some extraordinary circumstances to become ready for my instructor to show up. When I hit a level of readiness, the teacher did indeed appear in a truly remarkable fashion.

I have had numerous teachers during my life. Each one contributed in both negative and positive ways to the person that I have become. When the one who is the subject of this book arrived in my life, she changed me in deeply emotional ways that, even today, I am still trying to comprehend.

When one traditionally thinks of a teacher, a schoolhouse and formal classroom image might come to mind. However, some of the best teachers can take the learning out of the classroom and create a personalized curriculum tailored to the student's needs at that time. The best teachers will create an environment where the student can explore and discover the answers themselves, allowing them to learn by succeeding and failing. They are always there watching over the student, nudging them ever so subtly and there to catch them when they are about to fail.

My teacher dramatically spoke to me one night in a somewhat formal introduction. Since that time, my life has been one of the most amazing journeys and something that I could not have imagined had I wanted to. There have been so many twists and turns along the way, but I am constantly reminded that I am the student of the one who showers me with unconditional love. In fact, as you will see in the rest of this book, it is not something that does originate outside of one's self. It is only when we truly realize this that it can begin within. When people understand that they are love itself, and they share that love with each other, true love is expressed.

This book's title comes from the first thing she asked me during that initial interaction. After I chose that title, I realized that it has so many more layers to it. Now, I am asking you, the reader, if you hear my voice. By doing so, I am attempting to stand in my truth and share something incredibly special to me. I am becoming vulnerable in front of you and asking if you will take a moment to really listen to what I am saying, and take this journey with me.

If you peel back another layer and go deeper, this book is also a challenge to you. Are there aspects of your life where you just need to be heard? Do you need someone to just listen? Sometimes that is all we can ask. We just need that sympathetic ear, which will allow us to speak the truths in our hearts and be heard.

I hope this book becomes a testament to the many who are out there just waiting to listen and will give the reader the courage to ask, "Do you hear my voice?"

Chapter 1

A Quick Trip

A secret agenda

In September of 2019, I found myself standing alone in front of a grave of a woman that I had never met. Even today, just the idea that I would be standing there seems very unusual. I had never done anything like that. I had been sitting on an aluminum bench in a stadium at a Boise State University football game the night before. While I sat there enjoying the game with my freshman daughter, I thought back to the many hours that I had spent in that place as a child with my father, and later as a college student. Now, I was sharing the experience again with my daughter.

It was one of those moments when I just felt very connected to who I was and who I had become. It all came back to love, family, and shared experiences that created a bond. Still, I anticipated creating another memory with the quick trip that I would be making the following morning, and the events that led me to consider that journey were in the back of my mind.

I had flown to Boise from Seattle the morning of the game. Staying in the guest bedroom of some dear friends, I tossed and turned all night, anxious for the day after the Friday night game. I had not shared my covert plans with anyone. I felt as though they would think that I was crazy if they knew what I was doing. I decided that it would be better to disguise my reasons for going, so I made up a lame excuse about meeting with someone the following day.

The next morning, I arose before dawn so that I could try to make an eight-hour round trip to central Utah and be back to spend some additional time with my daughter and some other friends that evening. I jumped in my rental car just before 6 a.m. Morning dew covered the windows of the vehicle. For a while I sat in the car, waiting for the wipers, defrosters, and heaters to do their jobs before departing. I wanted my pilgrimage to begin.

Finally, I headed to the freeway. I only stopped briefly at a drive-through stand to get a large cold-brew coffee for the road. As I drove, I watched the majesty of the sky changing from star-speckled black to blue, and the horizon gradually transitioning from black to pink and then to yellow as the sun came up.

My mind, a flurry of thoughts, raced. I wondered what the moment would be like when I first saw the resting place for this woman whose spirit I had come to know over the past year. Would there be a grave marker? How would it look?

How would I feel at that moment? I felt so anxious, but at the same time, such a sense of peace.

Because of the beauty and serenity of the drive, at times, I found myself nodding off only to catch myself before entirely falling asleep at the wheel. The combination of lack of sleep and the peacefulness of the drive left me vulnerable. I stopped again to get an energy drink and kept driving. I felt determined to get to my destination. I had to get there and pay my respects.

When I arrived at the destination, I drove around, hoping to find someplace to buy flowers. My parents taught me at an early age that when you visit a gravesite, you should always take flowers as a sign of respect. It was a gorgeous early fall morning, complete with clear blue skies, a brightly shining sun, and the leaves on the trees beginning to change from green to yellow.

Except for some workers taking care of some new burial sites in the distance, I was alone in that cemetery section. Since I had scouted the exact location of her gravesite with a combination of Google Maps, Street View, and the cemetery's gravesite locator, I knew exactly where to go. It felt like I had been there before.

Even today, the story of how I got there seems both improbable and impossible. Still, there I was in the middle of Utah, placing a note and flowers on this individual's gravestone. The flowers I had just purchased, but the note was written and edited several times over the prior weeks. I wanted the contents to be generic enough that if read, the writer would not seem entirely out of his mind, but I also wanted to include information to show that it came from a loving place.

Once again, I felt afraid that others would think that I was crazy, but I was also secretly hoping to get caught at the grave to share my amazing story with someone who knew this woman before her death. The note said that I had come from miles and lifetimes away to honor the life that she lived. I wrote that I could not wait until we met on the other side of the veil and talked about all our experiences here on earth.

I am sure that any rational person may consider the story of what happened to me during the previous year, which led me to this moment, unlikely. There is nothing logical about this story, but that is also the beauty of it. Had I not experienced it myself, I may have laughed at it as being some delusional fantasy. Still, there I was standing before a gravestone, so far from my home in Washington.

The main reason for me being there was that a spirit named Jessica spoke to me early one morning a year prior, as I awoke from a dream. That set off a series of events that have led me to understand that unlikely as it may seem, I had an eternal connection with her that goes beyond anything that I could have imagined.

I have come to discover the immortality of the soul. Relationships and bonds that exist outside of this life can be significantly stronger and more profound than anything we can have on earth. Sometimes, that bond is so strong that it allows one soul to reach through the veil and aid someone on this side to correct their path, point them in the right direction, and help them find their way when they may be lost. I believe that is what happened to me, and this is that story, but it is also the story of how I came to understand everything that happened for me to be there at that time.

In a line from an old Nat King Cole song initially written by Eden Ahbez called "Nature Boy," he sings that one of the most important things we can learn in this life is love and accepting love from others.

Ultimately, this story is about love and how it transformed me and my perception of the universe.

Chapter 2

Conditional Connection to the Divine

How did I get here?

How does someone who grew up in a very conservative family, who were members of the Church of Jesus Christ of Latter-Day Saints (Mormons), end up believing that he has a special relationship with a dead woman, especially one whom he had never met during this life? That is an interesting story that spans over fifty years. It involves the way I was brought into this life and my early education. Still, more than that, it required me to learn about who I am and not who others expected me to be.

As an old friend once explained to me, everyone learns life lessons at different times in their lives. It took over half a century for me to open enough to be receptive to under-standing something that had always been there. This story will travel through some of my early life. It will also show that when I opened my heart and mind up, I met the people that I needed to meet at the exact moment when I needed them.

"You are a descendant of Abraham through the loins of Ephraim, and through that tremendous bloodline, you have the privilege and obligation to live and teach the gospel of Jesus Christ. You were sent here for a particular purpose, and as you keep the command-ments of God, this purpose will be made known unto you. Keep your mind and body clean and pure so that the Lord can guide you in the path of righteousness and truth all the days of your life."

That was the first paragraph from my Mormon "Patriarchal Blessing" given to me at eighteen years old. That blessing is only given by a man appointed and ordained by the local leadership to perform that function. I had to receive a rec-ommendation from my local bishop to even get in the door. This blessing is designed to guide and identify any unique gifts that one can obtain by following the church's teach-ings.

Looking back, it seemed more of an affirmation of every-thing the church and my parents had taught from birth. That is to say, I was chosen and obligated to be a member of the church. Adherence to a stringent set of rules and regulations created by the church's patriarchal leadership provided a person with a provisional ticket to a divine connection. Without that permission, one had no right even to expect that kind of relationship would even be a possibility.

As a young male in my sexual prime, I can honestly say that my mind and body were not always "clean and pure" in the way they defined it. It appeared that without being perfect, I could never fully have a personal relationship with God. I still fell short and eventually gave up trying.

For over fifty years, somewhere in the deepest portions of my mind, I considered myself unworthy of any kind of connection. Then one night, something incredibly powerful happened that began a series of events that helped me understand the connection was always there. I just had to clear debris collected from a lifetime of self-doubt.

For this story, I want to share the evolution of my belief system, momentous events, and the guidance that I have received along the way. When I discuss that church, I do not do so with the intent to criticize it. I only use it as an example of how my beliefs had to change to plug into an energy flow and a whole network of guides and teachers that aided me along my path.

Let us start at the beginning.

> "...having been born of goodly parents, therefore I was taught somewhat in all the learning of my father." *1 Nephi 1:1 (Book of Mormon)*

Born into membership in the Mormon church, I was the youngest of six children. Nearly twenty years separated my oldest sibling from me. At my birth, he had been preparing to go on a mission. My mother had labor induced to allow her the flexibility to go with my father and brother to Salt Lake City, to enter the Mission Home before he embarked on his mission to Germany.

Those were different times, and because I was a newborn, they thought that the trip would be too difficult for them and me, so they left me with a neighbor, a friend from church, and drove down. They had such devotion to the church that they would leave their newborn son with a neighbor to ensure that the older son entered the Mission Home to start his mission on schedule.

Looking back, I understand the difficulty of that decision for my parents, especially during that era. Still, I also know that decision to leave me has affected my need for approval from others in almost everything that I do. As a newborn, I was taken away from my mother, my only real attachment and connection to this earth, shortly after my birth, only to have her return a few days later. The woman I bonded with within the womb was suddenly not there, only to reappear a few days later.

That act seems so minor when looked at in the entirety of my life. Still, that separation and lack of initial attachment bonding had a significant effect on me. It must have confused me at the very least. I can just imagine my immature feelings, wondering what I did to make her leave? Equally, what did I do to make her come back?

My parents had given me a middle name that cemented my relationship with that church forever: Alma. They named me after the bishop of their ward (parish). The Prophet

Alma "wrote" the most extensive section of The Book of Mormon. When I later discovered that the name outside of the church is considered a girl's name, it became a source of shame for me. I found it embarrassing throughout my life when others discovered, or I had to reveal it. Why would my parents have cursed me with such a name? I hated that name. Even though it does mean "soul" in Spanish, it is one of those names that brought about ridicule from my peers.

More recently, a good friend told me that my parents unknowingly gave me a great blessing with that name. It is a constant reminder that I should be centered on my softer spiritual side. But I did not learn about that until much later in life.

The youngest of six kids with two devout parents, I grew up doing everything in the church. Besides playing with the neighborhood kids and visiting local relatives who were not church members, everything else seemed to revolve around church meetings and prescribed religious activities.

Originally, I attended at least two sessions on Sunday when I was younger and a three-hour block of meetings on Sundays later. The church also appointed Monday evenings as "Family Home Evening." On this night, the families would learn a gospel lesson and have a family activity. Many times, it seemed to be an occasion where the word "family" should have been replaced with the word "forced." I hated those evenings. My parents, especially my dad, really tried to do what the church had told him to do, but every Monday evening was such a struggle. We only did it because the church said we should. Tuesday evenings were for youth meetings. My parents always seemed to have Thursday night meetings, too. The church's concept seemed to be that if they keep the members overly involved, they would not have time to stray.

Being the youngest and feeling deep down inside that I was not good enough without parental and adult favor, I developed a great desire to please those around me. My parents' approval meant I was loved. With my father being an absolute believer, that meant that I would have to prove to him that I was worthy of his love by being a "good Mormon boy." I idolized him, and I sincerely believed all that he and the church taught.

Dad was the disciplinarian, and my mom, the more compassionate one. While I admired my dad, I still feared him. Any disapproval made his punishment seem much harsher. "I am so disappointed" stung just as much as the yardstick swatting my bare bottom.

Over time, I developed the mentality that I did not want to expose my defects, lack of devotion, or doubts to anyone in the church or my family. I always deferred to authority, even if I disagreed. I did not want the conflict. Doing what my parents and the church wanted, at least outwardly, became a way to avoid pain and rejection. I was far from perfect and always felt guilty and unworthy with the slightest misdeed. Deep down, the desire to prevent that perceived threat of punishment and rejection became far greater than the desire to do the right thing. In a twisted way, I based my value not on what I thought of myself but on how I perceived what others thought about me.

This feeling of unworthiness even seemed to extend to my dreams. In one repeated dream, Jesus was coming to my home. I was so excited. I saw him walking toward our house and I tried to turn on the front light so he could find me. The outside light did not turn on. Nothing I did could get that light fixture to work. When he could not find the house, he got into a taxi and left. I always thought that this dream meant that I was not worthy enough to meet Jesus. I kept coming back to the following Bible verse:

> "Let your light so shine before men, that they may see your good works, and glorify your Father which is in heaven." *Matthew 5:16*

I could not turn on my light, so Jesus could not see me. I failed at letting the light of Jesus shine from me, or so I thought. It was not until recently that I discovered that I had missed the real meaning of this dream.

During my teenage years, I would sneak off to the store and take sneak peeks at adult magazines and do other things that my parents and the church would not approve of, in secret, each time feeling further and further disconnected from my Divine source. Remember, with many religions, a person can only connect by following that sect's rules.

One time, I was caught stealing one of those magazines. I told my parents that it was a photography magazine because I was really interested in photography. I was now a thief and a liar, all the time imagining my relationship with Him getting weaker. However, I tried to maintain the image on the outside of the "good Mormon." My parents kept my theft quiet. I did have to tell the local bishop; my punishment was to not partake of the sacrament (communion) for one week.

I continued to perform the quiet kid's role, where I did not excel at anything but also never appeared to do any wrong. The kids who excelled or were overtly rebellious got all the attention. I did not want that, because they were set on a pedestal or observed more closely. I preferred not to have the spotlight in any capacity. That was for others; deep down inside, I felt that I was not worthy.

Any kind of conflict always seemed like torture, and I would do anything to avoid it. I found myself agreeing with philosophies and ideals that I did not believe in to prevent the pain of conflict, deferring rather than fighting, playing the diplomat and not the leader, and sitting in the back instead of the front. This "hiding" skill gave me a deep sense of internal pride, especially when I would hear compliments about what a good kid I was, but more importantly, it kept me out of trouble.

I went to all church activities and administered the sacrament, a duty of the priesthood. Most Mormon boys are ordained to the lesser priesthood at twelve. Thinking back, I should have received an acting award. I was not happy. However, I feared ever leaving the church. I worried about what my family and friends would think and say about me. I had heard the way they talked about others who left the church. There always seemed to be contempt in their voices.

Growing up, I continually heard and read stories like the "Iron Rod" in The Book of Mormon. The iron rod represented the gospel. Those who held onto the rod found the

Tree of Life and could partake of the fruit from the Tree. Those who let go of that rod were lost. And those who tasted the fruit and then left received the worst punishment, because they knew the truth and turned away from it.

I had a Sunday school teacher who related a personal experience that hammered this point home. He told us a story of a former missionary companion of his. This person, after his mission, had found another path and started to attend another church. He found his passion there and became a preacher. Some of his sermons even preached against his former religion. My teacher looked at us all directly in the eyes and said in a very stern voice, "He is going to hell. He knew the truth and turned away."

There I was, feeling guilty about everything, feeling no real connection to God, and terrified to leave. My acting ability became even more robust. I could, most of the time, push that guilt so far down that sometimes I did not think it was there, but I always knew the deep dark shadow lingered. Maybe if I ignored that shadow, it would disappear.

My entire social life and the church were intertwined because of the amount of time I spent there and in other church activities. All my close friends were there. This complicated relationship with the church, and left me spiritually shut off. I could not open my heart entirely to anyone. I built these high walls around me to keep others from knowing the truth about me.

I did go on a mission and kept myself active in the church for a while after that. I even became very judgmental of friends who had open vices that were different from mine. No one knew all of mine; add hypocrite to the list of vices keeping me from my spiritual connection.

I just wanted to keep everyone happy. I always thought that anything that I had to say might not matter, as others had probably already figured it out. I had no confidence in my voice, beliefs, and intuition. It took a long time to heal, and begin to regain the inner confidence I inherently deserved.

Chapter 3

Life Has No Meaning

"Since there is no meaning to life, I can be sad and depressed, or I can enjoy the hell out of the time that I have here." - Karthik

My path out of the Mormon church began in a class-room within the church during college. My instructor detailed out how we should be in the world, but not of the world. During his lecture, he said one thing that sped up my decision to leave the church. He said, "The problem with college is they teach you to question everything."

I am not sure why that one comment affected me so much, as I had grown up repeatedly hearing similar sentiments. This time, though, alarms started going off in my head, like those in war or sci-fi movies when a ship is about to be attacked. Was he telling us not to question anything that came from the church? To just accept that they know what is best for us at all times? "Are you serious?" I thought.

At that point, I knew that I did not belong, and I must find an exit. That exit was not as immediate as one may imagine, but a weaving path that brought me, at times, to straddle the fence between actively participating and ultimately leaving the church.

For my entire life, my social life had revolved around the church. I had very few close friends outside of it. With my friends in the church, there was no way that I could tell them how I was feeling. I could not express my innermost thoughts. So I began to reinforce my walls. How could I tell anyone in my immediate social circle that I doubted everything? Doubting was looked on as a weakness. Who could I tell that at one point, I even tried to commit suicide? Instead, I began to dip my toe in the water of life outside of that life.

One of my first adventures in pulling away was sneaking out to a local suburban dive bar. I thought no one would know me there, and I could try some alcohol with no one seeing me. I was an adult at that time. I had no reason to sneak around, except for the fear of being exposed as one of those people who did not follow the church policies.

That worked for a while, but then I was caught by a coworker. While at the bar, we politely shared greetings; it did not take him long to run back to those I worked with to tell them the news. I had that "good boy" reputation, so to see me drinking at a bar was just too good to hold. Now that the people at work knew, I began to get asked to join them after work. One of those coworkers eventually became one of my dearest friends, who has stuck by me through good times and bad. For that, I will be forever grateful for being caught at that dive bar.

The struggle to find my place in this world continued. I felt rudderless. I worked at multiple dead-end jobs, and the city where I lived did not seem to offer a lot of opportunities for me. At this point, I had in effect left the church, although it would be much later that I would have my records removed. I no longer attended meetings. I had made the break from believing in church doctrine. When I finally did ask to have my records removed years later, the church gave me a thirty-day period to consider my eternal salvation before they actually removed my name. I felt some initial guilt, but quickly got over it. Because of my parents' passion for the church, I never had the heart to tell them what I had done. I believe they must have known, but I never had the courage to tell them directly. Once again, even though I was a grown man, I lacked the courage to stand up for myself because I worried about how it would impact others.

I finally took a job as a teacher in a small town in Asia for six months, teaching English to kids and adults. It was challenging; I struggled to instruct the toddlers, as they did not understand me. During my off-hours, I met some other teachers who were not native to Asia, and we bonded. Much of my leisure time was spent within this small group.

I developed a strong relationship with one friend in particular, Karthik. The son of a college professor, he was born in India but grew up in Texas. We had some great in-depth conversations that ranged from football to politics to philosophy. He had a brilliant and insightful mind that forced me to not always accept the surface-level explanation, but look for deeper meaning.

We continued our friendship even after I left. About a year later, we did meet up again when I returned to Asia to attempt a magnificent around-the-world journey with him. The plan was for us to work our way through different countries, but this grand scheme fell apart in Japan when Tokyo ate up our reserve funds more quickly than we'd planned, and we became homeless. I ended up back in the States at my sister's home in Pennsylvania, and Karthik landed in India, where his sister lived. I thus began my Stateside struggle again to find my place in life.

Karthik eventually found his way back to the States, but in a different part of the country from me. We talked on the phone several times. In one of these conversations, he told me about India. At one point, he had spent several weeks at a Buddhist temple meditating on life. During that time, he had concluded that there was no meaning to life.

He spent his remaining time in the temple, extremely depressed. He thought that if there was no meaning to life, why was he struggling to survive? If we are born, live, and die, and that is it, why try? The depression deepened. One day while meditating, the thought came to Karthik that since there was no meaning to life, he could be sad and depressed, or he could enjoy the hell out of the time that he has here.

From that time forward, until recent years, I internally adopted my version of this philosophy. I did not believe in the existence of any higher power. If there was no higher power, I did not need a connection.

My purpose became, how do I get through this life and make it not hurt too much.

Chapter 4

From No Meaning
to Meaning

I want to learn more

I would say that I did not believe in much of anything for many years. If I could not taste, touch, see, hear, or feel it, how could it possibly be true. I think that I still wanted some sort of magic in the world, but I gave up looking.

After many years of keeping a distance from anything spiritual, my department at work became integrated within another division. One of the people I came to know in that division was Shelli, who, without knowing it at the time, helped me find my current path, including the belief that I do have a purpose on this earth and that my life does have meaning.

We initially began to have more in-depth conversations because of a positive mental attitude book that I had talked about with the divisional leadership. Soon I began having conversations with my new friend about keeping positive attitudes. She showed me some crystals that she kept at her desk, but I did not know what to think. I remember thinking that she was a little "out there," but accepted it because that was just part of the total package of who she was.

This woman never had any designs to change my beliefs, but I imagine that she is one of those souls who showed up on my path when I most needed them, even if I was not looking for them. Over the years, Shelli has become a quiet guide and counselor. She is someone who will put a jewel in my pathway and in her way, say, "Look at that jewel on the path ahead." Then she says no more. When I go down the path to pick up and examine the jewel, I will see its beauty and admire it. When I am feeling thankful for having had the opportunity to partake in the beauty of that stone, I hear her voice saying, "I know that is pretty, but you should see the stone that is further down the path." And once again, I head down a path of discovery.

This gift comes so naturally that I am not sure that Shelli even realizes what she does, but this has happened so often that I have come to greatly value and trust her intuition and our relationship. She has sent me down such amazing roads, each time finding new "jewels" of beauty and wisdom.

The first two gems that she placed in my path were Michael Sheridan's dream interpretation work, and a local meetup called Wisdom Soup.

I had always been fascinated by my dreams. Besides the previously mentioned Jesus dream, as a young man I had repeated dreams of being on stage at a rock concert, where someone handed me an electric guitar and I could play it flawlessly. I would always be disappointed upon waking that that ability did not carry over into my waking life. After college, I would have many dreams of taking college exams on subjects I had never studied. Flying on a swing that was not physically attached to anything also often appeared. I even had one where I gave birth to a baby. The impossibility of these things made them even more intriguing. I wanted to know what they meant but never found a satisfactory explanation. None of the dream dictionaries could adequately describe what was happening in the dreams, or the emotions I'd experience.

One day at work, Shelli told me about a meetup that she attended where Michael Sheridan spoke. She told me about some of the interpretations that he had made for some of those who had attended. I became curious and wanted to find out more. I'd had many dreams in which my deceased parents would appear as actors, and I wanted to understand them. Were my parents trying to tell me something from the grave? Why did I have those dreams? I bought Michael's book *How to Interpret Your Dreams* and began to devour it.

I had never been to a meetup, always mistakenly thinking that they were some way for young singles to meet. Still, the idea of attending a meeting where I could learn more about this spirituality that I sensed growing within me intrigued me. In December 2017, I attended my first meetup. As I walked in, the creator of Wisdom Soup, Anne, greeted me and thanked me for attending. I felt welcomed at once but also felt very out of place. Part of me wanted to run away, and part wanted to stay.

It is easy to investigate these kinds of things on the internet in the privacy of one's home, but it is much more difficult to hide once you meet people. This was a community of people, and based on my past experience, it meant that someone could exercise control over my life. This would lead me to agree to things to appease those in power. I had spent so much of my life rebelling from that aspect of my life that I was not sure that I wanted to take the huge leap to join a new community. Even though looking back it was more like a small baby step, at the time, it was a significant jump into the unknown. Luckily, none of my fears were validated.

The title of this meetup was "Activate Your Desires for 2018 in the Field of Creation Resonance." A woman named Sheila led the discussion that taught us about the universe's resonant frequencies and how we could set our intentions, much like planting a seed and letting it grow. I was intrigued by the concepts that she taught, and by the end of the evening, I set my first real intention. I wrote, "I want to learn more about my spirituality and determine if I have any gifts."

I doubted that it would have any impact. How could writing and speaking something so simple have an impact? I had no idea the power that simple, pure intention would have over the trajectory of my life. It did not take long for me to get my first taste of the fruit of that intention.

Michael Sheridan, as mentioned previously, is an author, coach, and interpreter of dreams, and has spoken at this meetup a few times. I consider his gifts to be much like Joseph of the Bible, who could interpret the true spiritual meanings in dreams. Through his dream interpretations, I have found out what some of my spiritual gifts are and the obstacles to using those gifts. By working through those obstacles, I have been able to develop my gifts. As he often says, "The bumps are not in the way, they are the way."

As I was reading Michael's book, I had a dream. This one seemed vivid, and I felt a need to understand its meaning. I tried to use the book to interpret the contents, but being a novice at this kind of thing, I reached out to Michael for help. Here is a man who has had thousands of paying clients and appeared on television and radio, and I was asking him for help. At the time, I did not realize what a big deal it was or what a fantastic and humble person he is. Later he told me that there was something uniquely intriguing about this dream, and he decided to aid me.

In the dream, there were many symbols of karma that I needed to work out, ones that indicated that I had a strong intuition and channeling gifts. Mostly because I did not trust them or feel worthy of them, I did not recognize that they were there. Much of that I can trace back to my upbringing, where there seemed to be religious tests to prove myself worthy of receiving information from Source. I also discovered that I had guides that were waiting to provide me assistance along my path. In the dream, this was all packaged and presented with beautiful symbolism.

At the end of the dream, I also learned the importance of not accepting others' karmic debt or trying to pass my own to anyone else, and that working off my debt was vital in progressing forward with my soul's path. When one tries to take shortcuts or bypass debt, they just incur more debt and prolong the journey. Unless you enjoy that struggle, that may not be the best way. (The full dream and Michael's interpretation are available in the Appendix at the end of this book.)

After reading Michael's in-depth interpretation of that dream, I knew and felt deep within me that he had a true gift. My dreams were somehow the key to helping me on my path. For the first time in my life, I had found a person who could help me understand my dreams and exactly what they meant.

More importantly, I began to realize that I had a unique path within me. I was not living to fulfill someone else's path, but my own. I had contributions that I needed to make to others and this world that were exclusively mine. I may not have fully understood then, but this dream launched my spiritual quest, one that would eventually lead me to a spiritual relationship I could not have imagined.

Later that spring, Shelli put another gem in my pathway. After Michael interpreted that dream in early January 2018, I realized that my dreams indicated strong channeling ability, but I wondered how this could be true. Much like the distant radio connection, I could not really understand the messages I was receiving, or if I was really getting anything. I have come to realize that channeling is just another word for what many religions call "inspiration," or listening to the "still, small voice inside," or having the Holy Ghost guide you.

I have a friend who is a talented singer and songwriter, and he often tells me that his best songs will come to him in a flash. It is the same thing. That inspiration was what I had felt so disconnected from throughout most of my life. When Shelli told me about a channeling class that she was attending on Sunday evenings, I thought, "Wow, there is someone who can teach me how to do this?"

I must say that going into the class, I was skeptical, primarily because the concept of channeling had never resonated with me. Whenever I had encountered that concept before, I had been told that it was evil, the people who did that were all fakes, and it must be some sort of act to deceive vulnerable people to make money. I was interested because it was taboo, but I also thought, "What if it is real? Wouldn't that be cool?"

The teacher, Heidi, was an extremely talented channel, and I was interested to see how it worked, but at the same time I worried that I would not be able to connect and would make a fool of myself. Or maybe I would realize that it all really was fake. Once again, it felt as though I was about to make another major leap, only to discover that it was just another baby step forward.

This class was virtual and used video conferencing technology. Usually, there would be at least five to six of us that would call in. After a connection and grounding meditation, the teacher would begin the class by asking if anyone had any questions that they wanted to ask the group. These questions ranged from "What is my life purpose" to "Am I on the right path" to "Should I quit my job?"

The class would then try to connect and channel an answer. At first, I would get nothing. Later, that turned into flashes of a picture, which I discounted every time as not being truthful information. Being an excellent channel, Heidi knew who in the class was receiving messages and would call on that person to share what they had felt or seen. When she called on me the panic would appear, but as I learned to not filter and just say what I felt, heard, or saw, a deeper understanding of the process began.

One evening, a woman in the class asked if we could connect to her brother, who had recently died. As I tried to connect, I immediately became overwhelmed with real weight and a sense of remorse. I was terrified of what I was feeling. I sensed that her brother had chosen his exit from the earth. Because I did not understand what I was feeling, I did not tell the class about it. I remember hearing a voice tell me to let his sister know that he was okay and in a good place now, which I did. Later, the woman let the class know that her brother had committed suicide, and she told me that what I had said to her that night sounded exactly like what her brother would say.

That summer, I continued the pursuit of all things spiritual. I meditated more, and started keeping a journal of all my experiences. I worked with Michael to better understand my dreams and what they were trying to tell me, and continued attending the channeling classes. I also worked with

Catherine, a gifted shadow worker, to understand and embrace some of the past's shadows blocking my path.

Most of the time outside of work was spent learning and pursuing a spiritual and healing path. Things suddenly took a powerful turn when I had a particular dream that changed my life.

Chapter 5

The Dream That Changed My Life

Trust your heart and not your head

Many people have moments in their lives that they can point to as a turning point that defines who they will become or a path that they will take. Mine was a dream and, more specifically, what happened upon waking from it. I had no idea that one simple dream could set off a chain of events that would change my life. I had learned from Michael that each dream is significant, and I was paying attention to all of them to learn more about myself.

On its own, there was nothing significant about this dream; it was like many that I'd had before. It began at a pristine mountain lake, the water so clear that if you looked at it from the right angle, you might wonder if it was there. Granite rocks of all sizes surrounded the water and continued down to the very bottom. The lake looked like one of the many that I had visited as a kid backpacking with my family in the Sawtooth Wilderness Area in central Idaho. It seemed so familiar. The difference now was I was all alone, and around the lake I saw twenty huge photos, each one about 6'x8'. Just like a painter's canvas, each photo seemed to be supported by a lightweight frame.

Somehow, I knew that I had been assigned a task to arrange these pictures in a particular order. Still, even though I understood that was what I had to do, I had no instructions on how to do it or what the correct order was. In the dream, I moved these photos around all day long, placing this photo with that one to try different combinations. I tried everything that I could think of to figure it out; it was a puzzle that needed to be solved.

After much trial and error, at about dusk, I finally succeeded. I felt such relief and pride that I had solved the puzzle. As I reveled in my victory, a voice spoke to me in an almost condescending manner. It said, "Trust your heart and not your head."

What? No, "Excellent job" or "Attaboy"? Up until that moment, I had been proud of my accomplishment, but all I got was, "Trust your heart and not your head." Really?

I must not have learned my lesson, because this dream kept repeating itself that night on a loop; it felt like a *Groundhog's Day* situation. Each time it was the same lake, the same twenty photos, the same task, and in the end, the same voice would speak. I was caught in a vicious loop that I could not escape.

"Trust your heart and not your head."

I became increasingly frustrated but would always hear the same voice. I was angry. I just wanted to quit. Why wouldn't this just end? The thought of doing it one more time seemed unbearable, and I felt total despair. I was defeated; the lake had won. A sense of hopelessness overcame me.

Finally, I looked down and saw the same scene again. I could not imagine doing it all over again. In complete surrender, I thought, "Let me try this heart thing." And the photos magically went into the right order on the first try. This amazing feeling of victory came over me. I had finally won.

I immediately woke up from that dream. I looked at my phone. It was 2:10 a.m. on September 24, 2018. My first thought was that the message in this dream was unmistakable. I would not need Michael's help to determine the meaning of this one.

I tried to get back to sleep. It was a Monday morning, and my alarm was set for 5 a.m. I needed to sleep. As I lay there, I suddenly heard a voice. I had never experienced an unknown voice at night, and this voice was so different from anything that I had ever heard before. Each word sounded like a forward track layered over a reverse track of the same word, and I could hear each word coming at me before it arrived. I find it difficult to describe the sound of that voice because it was so unique. The room's feeling also changed to a different kind of energy, one that was very distinctive.

The voice said, "My name is Jessica _____. I will be guiding you through the next phase of your life. Do you hear my voice?" She had offered both her first and last name, which seemed odd.

I looked around, trying to figure out to whom she was talking. When I realized that it was me, I said, "Yes."

Then she asked, "It is different from yours, right? Can you hear the difference?"

"Yes, I can."

"When you hear this voice, you will know that it is not you, but me talking to you. I want you to remember it. It will be very important."

Then the voice was gone. Lying there in shock, I wondered what had just happened. I felt something remarkable had just occurred but could not make sense of it. I was not sure what to think. Was Jessica a real spirit guide or angel? I had never heard of a spirit guide introducing themselves like that, especially talking directly to me. Was she a rogue spirit with some nefarious designs trying to gain my confidence? Or was it just some sort of a pre-dawn auditory hallucination? I did not know.

Hearing voices in the night, when completely alert, was a very new experience for me. In hindsight, I wish that I would have had the presence of mind to start asking her questions at that time. It would have saved me a lot of trouble, but then again, the path to understanding would not have been as interesting. Instead, I lay there bewildered, not knowing what to think or do.

My adrenaline was pumping. There was no way I would be able to sleep, having no reference for what had just happened. That kind of visitation did not appear to be normal. I kept going back and forth between "good" or "bad" because I could only reference night visitations in those terms; from my upbringing, it was an either/or situation. When referring to spirits, only two choices existed in my mind. I needed to get answers about what had just happened.

Luckily, I had a session with Michael a couple of days later. I sent my dream to him in advance. When I told him about the dream, I included the story of Jessica speaking to me after it ended. I asked him who Jessica was. I did not ask him about the dream itself, as I had a clear understanding of its message. He said that she appeared to be a newer low-level spirit guide who was learning, and not to worry because experienced guides were backing her up and wouldn't let her make a mistake.

I was not sure what to take from that. My immediate thought was one of frustration. With all the work and investment in time and money that I had made over the last several months, did that only qualify me for a "low-level" guide? I felt that I had been making such great strides and had come a long way. My dreams told me that I had many spiritual gifts, and here I was being informed that I only got a trainee guide? How could that be right? I felt so discouraged.

As I pondered what he really meant, he asked when my next channeling class was. I told him that it was the following Sunday. He said that I should ask Heidi about Jessica, as she was much better at channeling this kind of information than he. That gave me some hope, but I expected to just get confirmation around Michael's explanation that she was a new guide.

The following Sunday, I could not wait for the virtual class to begin. After a beginning meditation, the teacher asked if any of us had questions to ask the class to practice our channeling. I said that I had two. One was about Jessica, and the other about ties with my mother. Even before the lake dream, I had had dreams about the trauma that I had experienced as a newborn when my mother had left me with a neighbor shortly after birth. As previously mentioned, I never fully bonded with her during that critical time right after birth.

I was quite nervous as I began to tell the class about Jessica. My words became twisted, and to this day, I am not sure just how I got my first question out, but somehow, I did. The core of my question was, who or what was Jessica? We went around the class and asked if anyone was receiving any messages. Several of the classmates confirmed what Michael had told me. Yes, Jessica was indeed a guide to me, which was comforting, but frustrating as it gave me no real understanding of what had happened.

Then Heidi spoke. One of the unique things about her is that she could tap into something at a much higher level. She said that while she did not fully understand the concept, the guides told her Jessica was a "twin flame." She suggested that I do an internet search to learn more about that. I wrote those two words on a notepad that was sitting on my desk. I had never heard of such a thing, and had no clue as to what it could be. But my connection with Jessica seemed to be more than that of just a guide.

I then asked my second question, regarding my mother. The class suggested that I work with someone who could deal with trauma issues and gave me several suggestions. But honestly, I could not wait for the call to end just to find out what this twin flame thing was about. That seemed so much more important.

As soon as the call finished, I clicked on my browser and typed "twin flame" in the search bar. What came up seemed like a lot of far-fetched stories. Many people claimed to have twin flames. Most seemed to be convinced they shared that specific connection with each new person they met. To me, it appeared as though "twin flame" was the new "soul mate."

I can say that what I have experienced as a twin flame is quite different from ninety percent of what I read that night. Maybe I use the term incorrectly and what I have felt with Jessica is different and not exactly a twin flame in its purest sense, but most online stories didn't resonate with me.

After a lot of searching, I finally came across some descriptions that began to make sense. I pieced together the following description. Twin flames come from a single soul whose energy at one point in its evolution grew so much that the soul divided into two mirror images, one carrying more masculine energy and the other mostly feminine. Generally, they do not live in the same plane of existence or time. Still, because they were initially one soul, the draw to reunite is incredibly powerful. Even though some are rarely together, that attraction remains. Sometimes one twin takes on a physical form while the other stays in the Spirit world. When this happens, communication is challenging, but the love connection can be stronger. These two souls are bonded through a passion that penetrates the very core of their essence.

After reading those descriptions, I closed my laptop and thought, "Cool, I have a twin flame."

In my mind, I thought I had some new aspects of my spirituality that I could explore. I had no clue what this meant, or how much it would come to mean to me. I could not have imagined how knowing about my connection would change my life, but I was about to find out.

Chapter 6

My Connection to Jessica

This intense feeling of being loved

I arose the next day, just one week after my visit from Jessica. The alarm went off at 5 a.m., and I dragged myself out of bed. I had not gotten much sleep the night before because I had pondered about twin flames and Jessica and just what it could all mean. As with any other Monday morning, I prepared for work. I brewed my morning coffee to take with me. I took a shower and got dressed for the day.

But as I reached for my toothbrush, I heard Olivia Newton-John singing the most important lyrics from "I Honestly Love You" in my head, just as clear as it would be coming from my earbuds. The lyrics were about how much and how sincerely she loved me.

"Whoa, what was that? That was very random. Where did that come from?" I thought.

Then boom, it hit me. All the events of the last week seem to condense into one arrow tip of a thought. "Could this be Jessica reaching out to tell me what our connection means now that I know the 'twin flame' concept?" The impact of the thought pierced my heart. This connection seemed so new, but also in a way, so strangely familiar.

Now I had a mystery to solve. In reality, who was Jessica? Despite sensing these feelings, I felt bewildered. How could any of this be true, and who was this person?

That day I was useless. All morning I could only think about her. Who was she? Why now? I found it extremely difficult to concentrate on work. My first thought was that Jessica was possibly living, and we just had some astral plane connection. Because she had given me both her first and last name in our initial meeting, I began to look for living Jessicas on the internet. I got the feeling I may be looking in the wrong direction.

Then I remembered what Michael had said to me, and started thinking that if she was a new spirit guide, maybe she had died within the last several years. I began to search obituaries from the previous few years for every Jessica I could find, because I needed to find out more about her, even if it was her former self.

As mentioned, I did not initially understand why at our first meeting she had given me both her first and last name, but I did at that moment. It made the search so much more manageable. Because she still has living relatives, I have and will always protect her full name. It also does not fully define her eternal soul's essence.

As I searched online, I discovered many obituaries of women who shared her name who had passed on in recent years, some young, some old — each with her unique contribution to the earth and those around her. Then I came across one, and there was something about the woman's personality described there that connected with me. Maybe it was the sense of love that exuded from the portrait of her life, or perhaps some key qualities of the person portrayed. I am not sure, but I felt a connection immediately and viscerally.

The article had a photo attached. I also found other images of her. An old soul quality to her eyes and a depth of beauty at once drew me to them. They seemed to emanate an innate kind of love. Still, at the same time, I could sense a complex set of emotions lying just below the surface, almost like the delicate interplay of colors at sunset while knowing night would be there soon. Maybe what I saw in her eyes was more a reflection of me, or possibly it was the very humanity of them that allowed me to feel a connection. Whatever it was, I could not get the thought of this woman out of my mind.

At the same time, I convinced myself that my imagination had gotten the best of me. Who in their right mind thinks they have a connection with a dead woman, particularly one they have never met, and especially one they found online? Who really does that?

However, when I returned home that night and was finally alone, I started thinking of her again, not that I ever really stopped. I could not shake the thought of this woman. She consumed my mind. Even when I had no direct thoughts of her, feelings seemed to linger in the background. I did not know why. Why would I have any connection to this person? She was dead. I had never had any connection to her. We had only been within one hundred miles of each other three or four times at most during her life.

In the evening, when I found myself alone, the thoughts of this woman increased to the point where I found myself sheepishly calling out to her and asking if she was the one that I had found online earlier.

I was surprised to receive a response, in the same unique voice I had heard a week prior, the one she had so painstakingly told me to remember. I heard, "Yeah, that was me." The voice was undeniable. I had my confirmation.

More than that, suddenly, I felt overwhelmed with this intense feeling of being completely loved. It seemed to vibrate throughout my entire body. The sensation was so strong that it almost felt as though it even surpassed the word "love." It was such a powerful moment and one I had never experienced before. I felt completely consumed by this sensation, safe, and immersed in a feeling like stepping into an outdoor hot tub on a cold winter's night. I had a deep sense of peace I had never felt before.

That night I had a dream where Jessica and I were on a stage, creating abstract sculptures out of photos of my life. Thousands of pictures hung from three sculptures. We seemed to be having a fun time working on this project. Before we finished, we also created two more sculptures of the Archangels Gabriel and Uriel.

I later asked Michael what that meant. He said, "The dream shows her helping you get the most positive results out of your life. The stage is about being a messenger, as both Gabriel and Uriel relay messages to humankind. Statues represent ideals, so this co-creation means she is intrinsically involved in helping you realize the best in you."

Jessica was involved in helping me realize the best in me. Wow!

The next morning, I found myself downloading Olivia Newton John's "I Honestly Love You." I never really liked the singer or the song, but I listened to it as I drove to work. Tears started flowing when I heard one line about how her message came from her heart and not her head. I remembered the dream I was having just before Jessica first spoke to me, and the phrase that the dream pounded into my head over and over that night.

"Trust your heart and not your head."

The tears streamed down my cheeks, making it increasingly difficult to see the road ahead. Suddenly, I noticed a vibration in the palm of my right hand that was at first almost imperceptible, but then grew stronger. My fingers inexplicably curled up around the vibration. There almost seemed to be some weight to it, too. I realized Jessica and I were holding hands as I drove down the road.

The powerful feeling from the night before then flowed up my spine and consumed my body, but it was even more intense this time. It felt like it penetrated to the core of my soul. Words fail me when I try to describe that feeling. The closest is being wrapped in a warm quilt by someone you love and knowing you are completely safe with no worries in the world. I basked in the feeling for the rest of my commute. When I arrived at work, I sat in my car for a while, trying to gain my composure. It took several minutes, but I was able to go in and begin my work.

Later in the day, my head started trying to take control of the situation. It almost seemed as though it needed to be in charge and was very tired of all this "emotional goo." The questions and commentary started firing off, as if being shot from a machine gun.

"What the hell are you thinking?"

"All of these thoughts you are having are ridiculous. You know that, right?"

"You do realize she is dead, right?"

"You do realize you have never met her, don't you?"

"You know she will never be with you in this life, right?"

"This is so ridiculous; how will you ever explain this to anyone?"

"How can you even believe any of this?"

Then the heart would come back. "I have never felt anything this beautiful before. These past few days have been such an amazing experience. How can I turn my back on it?"

Then the head would fire back: "Dude! I have known you since you were born, and I am here to tell you that you are crazy!"

I seriously questioned my sanity. I had this whole heart-head tug-of-war going, and at the same time, I was trying to understand this enigma named Jessica. I continually struggled, thinking that I might be falling into a pit of insanity from which I may never come out. I felt terrified of the whole experience being false, but even more frightened that it could be true.

For several days I went back and forth, and the entire time I felt isolated, alone, and scared. Did I need counseling? I did not have any friends or family who would believe or understand what I was going through. I was alone. I could feel Jessica's constant presence, but that kept creating even more questions. I was very disoriented, and scared.

Chapter 7

Beginning to Heal the Past

A sense of sheer panic and loneliness

Even before Jessica spoke to me, I had realized that at some point, I would have to deal with the shadow of my mother briefly abandoning me after my birth. I thought that Catherine, the previously mentioned shadow worker, was the best person to help me. Earlier in the summer I had worked with her, and I learned not to ignore the shadows from my past but to explore and integrate them as part of me. When a person no longer hides from those past traumas but accepts them, the healing can begin.

Later in the week after meeting Jessica, I had an appointment with Catherine to try and heal the issues with my mother. At the time, I was not sure why it seemed so important to take care of it then, but it felt urgent.

One week prior to Jessica's introduction, I had had a dream where I was walking with my mother down a path. We saw a little girl's pink carry-on roller bag ahead. Unexpectedly, my mother shoved the bag off the trail and down into some bushes. I was confused about why my loving mother would do something like that.

Later in the dream, the little girl to whom the bag belonged was riding a train with her friend. Much like a subway, there was no real seating. The train became increasingly crowded, and the two girls became separated. I could see everything from the first girl's perspective, and as the train pulled away, I saw the doors close with the first girl still inside and the other child standing on the platform. A sense of sheer panic and loneliness filled me.

With Michael's help, I confirmed that I was the little girl in the train, separated from her friend on the platform. Even as I write this, I can still feel the terror and complete alone-ness that I felt at that moment. I was being sent to the lower vibrational human experience, and I could not take my best friend with me. It felt as though my heart was being ripped out of my body. I experienced a kind of despair and hope-lessness that I had never felt before.

We all have both male and female energy. The feminine side manifests as a spiritual connection, empathy, and intuition. My mother shoving the bag off the trail represented her leaving me with a neighbor shortly after birth, damaging that energy. That is what I needed to repair, and that is why I made the appointment with Catherine.

But Catherine also helped me learn about the girl I had left on the platform, who was the soul of Jessica.

I arrived early for the appointment, and I shared with Catherine the experiences of the previous two weeks. She commented on how my energy was different. It looked more "complete" than it ever had before. When she saw me, she said it appeared as though my spirit and Jessica's were connected. She also indicated that her office was full of spirit energy and more crowded than ever.

I excused myself and took a break to visit the restroom. When I returned, Catherine let me know that she had been talking to Jessica. She wanted to verify that my visitor was indeed who she purported to be. It comforted me to know that Catherine was there to protect me too.

We got started. The energy in the room seemed very elevated. At times it felt, as I wrote in my journal, as though we were in the middle of a cosmic cyclone with her standing over me, healing me while protecting me from the storm. Suddenly, I felt the strong presence of my mother, who had passed on about a year and a half prior. Catherine did too. She spoke with my mom and told her politely that this night was all about "healing Bruce." Even though she may feel bad about what she did, she needed to step aside and let the healing be focused on me.

With Catherine's guidance, I had to get to a place where I was emotionally that infant again to have the healing. In the middle of trying to heal the wounds from that experience, Catherine looked down at me and said, "Jessica just spoke to me."

It felt like my heart was going to stop. She told me that Jessica had explained an added trauma that I had experienced at my birth, of which I was unaware. I have previously mentioned that my mother induced labor to make me arrive early on this earth. The additional trauma was that I was pulled away from Jessica before I was ready, and just like the two girls on the train in the dream, I was abruptly separated from her in the spirit world. I felt I had no control. Then I was separated from my mother immediately after my birth. With both traumatic separations, I must have felt incredibly lost and alone.

Upon hearing all of this, just like a giant jigsaw puzzle the pieces magically went into their proper order, and I realized that I could do whatever I needed to do to heal from both traumatic experiences. I realized later that this was just the first step on the road to recovery.

Jessica had to come back to me at the precise time I needed her to help me connect the dots and begin to cut the ties with my mom and that traumatic experience. She was there at my birth and knew what happened, and was the only one who could have given that information to Catherine because she was a personal witness. Also, Catherine did not know about the dream that I had had the week prior.

At the end of the session, the energy in the room calmed. I felt liberated from all the trauma. She performed a ceremony to release any residual energy, and I felt free.

As I left, I got in the car and as is my practice, I put my phone's music player on random; I call it "music roulette." This time it seemed as though Jessica selected a song as

I pulled onto the freeway and started to accelerate: Van Halen's "Jump." Such a freeing song, and it perfectly matched my mood. She and I were definitely celebrating.

In the back of my mind, I started to worry that just as happiness seems to be always fleeting, now that Jessica was finished with her mission, would she be leaving me again too? Would I have to face the trauma of being left alone again? Although there was not a sign that would happen, I was unsure.

She had come back to me to help me overcome the past trauma, but was that her only mission, and now that she'd completed it would she move on? What happened later would help me overcome that fear.

Chapter 8

Walking into the Light - My First Lessons in Helping Lost Souls

A darkened room and a bright light

A few weeks after that night, Jessica turned into a teacher. She wanted me to learn, or rather she wanted to remind me, how some spirits do not always pass over into the light at death and that I could help those lost or stuck souls cross over with her assistance. What she taught me surprised me.

I did not realize at the time that this was not the first lifetime where Jessica had taught me about crossing into the light. Recently, I discovered that Jessica and I crossed paths in other lives too. One of those was during World War I. The image of what happened came through so clearly and vividly that it had to be real.

I was a young English soldier from Bristol laying on a cot in a dark country church in rural France, the chapel illuminated by only candles. I looked down and noticed the gaping hole in my abdomen. Blood oozed out of the wound. I felt so scared. I was shaking and trying to figure out just what happened to me. What was I doing in this old moldy-smelling church in the middle of France? Doctors were scurrying around, tending to other soldiers who screamed in agony. The feeling of death was ever-present. The events that led to that moment seemed hazy. I was in shock.

As I lay there, the most beautiful nurse I had ever seen sat down next to me and grabbed my hand. When she did, I immediately felt a sense of peace, and I somehow knew everything would be okay. When I experienced that scene again in my current life, I realized just who that nurse was. As she sat there holding my hand, she began to guide me toward the light. She knew that the end of my life approached quickly. As I moved toward the light, I felt her continuing to hold my hand and coaching me tenderly through each step of the path. I felt such a loving presence. When we arrived at the light, she wished me well and told me that we would see each other soon, and I walked into that glorious light.

One fall morning on the way to work, I could feel Jessica was with me. My average morning commute took about forty-five minutes, and about halfway, there was a T-intersection. I always turned left onto a very congested two-lane road. If you could go more than ten mph, you would be lucky. That day was no exception.

That morning I was first in line, stopped at that T-intersection and waiting for the light to change. I looked across the way and saw the big yellow sign with an arrow that pointed both left and right, but suddenly I felt a presence standing in front of the sign. I could not see him, but I felt him. In my mind, I knew that there was something there, even though I could not visually perceive what it was.

I dismissed it as my imagination. The light changed, and I turned the corner. Immediately after turning, I felt the presence again standing by the side of the road. I ignored him. Then 100 feet later, there he was again. I traveled another hundred feet, and the presence appeared again. I went further; the spirit was there again. Finally, I decided to talk to him.

I invited him into the car. I had no idea what I was doing. Now, I look back and wonder why I had been so naïve. Because I had watched ghost stories on television, I knew that I did not want him clinging to me, because in my mind, the worst thing that could happen would be to be possessed by a spirit that I met by the side of the road. I quickly set up some ground rules for our interaction. I told him that I had about a twenty-minute drive to my office from that point, and after that, we would have to go our separate ways. I did not want to have him attached to me. He agreed.

I then inquired why he wanted to talk with me. He explained in a sorrowful voice that he just wanted to go home. The emotions that I felt were that of a desperate man just trying to go somewhere, and he did not know how to get there. I am not sure how, but I realized that he was referring to his physical earthly home. I told him that that option was not available for him since he was dead. He then repeated that he just wanted to go home. He wanted his old life back.

Somehow, I realized that he needed to go into the light. I questioned each one of my thoughts. In the back of my mind, I had no idea if this could actually be happening. How could I be driving down the road, talking to a dead man who was sitting in the passenger seat with Jessica sitting in the back? What was going on here?

I then went into a long explanation about why he needed to go into the light, using everything that I had ever seen, heard, or read about it. What he told me next shocked me. He said, "I don't know how."

In my mind, I thought, "What do you mean you don't know how?" I felt that all he had to do was to walk into the light. It was simple. I wondered why he could not just go. From everything I'd ever heard, when someone dies, the light appears, and they walk through it. Why couldn't this man find the portal?

Suddenly, in my mind's eye, I could see a darkened room. There was a closed door on one end with a bright light shining around the edges. I told the man to go through the door. He then said that he did not know how to open it. Then I remembered that I had Jessica with me and thought, "Surely she knows how to get the door open. She must have done it before." At that time, I had no recollection that she had actually taken me there in the WWI life, so of course she knew.

I asked her if she could open the door, and she agreed to help the man. Then I saw her open the door, and a bright light illuminated the room. The man went to the door, paused, talked to Jessica for a moment, and then walked into the brightness. I felt Jessica's presence come back to the car, and she told me that he had been unsure whether or not to go into the light, as he was still holding out hope that he could go back to his old life. But then he decided he had no choice, and walked into the afterlife to begin the next phase of his journey.

When I realized what had just happened, I felt an adrenaline-like surge of energy explode through my body. It was such a profound feeling to know that I actually assisted someone in crossing into the light. Later, I found a news article about a man that had died in that area nearly two years prior. Somehow, I knew that was him.

After that, these occurrences became commonplace for a while. It was as though I was being exposed to all types of these souls who were caught in transition. Two of my favorite spirits that we helped cross over were an ex-high school wrestler and an old farmer. The high school wrestler was so happy to finally find the portal that he took a front flip through the door after Jessica opened it for him, because he was thrilled to be moving on. The old farmer kept shaking his head and laughing because of the perceived reprimand that he was about to receive from his wife for missing the light the first time. He kept saying that when he initially saw the light, he turned around to check on the dog. After he found the dog and confirmed that she was okay, he turned around again and "couldn't find the darned light again."

One evening when I first started to help these souls, I began to feel overconfident about my newly found gift. I began taunting the spirits by thinking, "You can't touch me. I have power over you."

Let me say that if someone wants to work with lost souls, this may not be the best thing to say. That night my room filled with spirits swirling around, getting in my face and taunting me. One of these spirits appeared to be demonic. Slowly but surely, I got them to leave, except for the one that seemed to be demonic. He would not go and would get right up to my face. He was different because he was trying to intimidate me. As he got closer to me, I noticed that his face was a mask. When I told him to take off the mask, his courage melted away, and he left my room.

What did I learn from this? Do not taunt spirits. I have come to realize that I am entering *their* world. They may not initially understand why I am there. If I walk into their world and immediately make demands of them, they will not trust me and will likely become agitated at my presence.

I learned to never trivialize the experience. The function of assisting someone in transition from the state of limbo to where they need to be is a sacred experience and should never be taken lightly. I am very humbled by the fact that I have been able to participate in that process.

I also learned I must always first protect myself before performing any of these services. Many of these lost souls have spent years deceiving themselves and creating a false reality about where they are and why they are in the limbo state. They can attack out of fear or pain, so it becomes especially important to create a safe space to work.

I learned I must control my thoughts when working with these souls. If I am not careful, these spirits can move from myself to others in their search for help. Once, while working with a lost spirit, I had a simple thought about another friend. I wondered if he had ever had a similar experience. That is all it took for one of the nearby spirits to find him; he ended up having to clear that spirit from him as it tried to attach itself to him.

More souls began to come to me for help. I had the feeling that Jessica was in the background organizing each experience that I had, or at least she was a great recruiter. I learned a lot about the process during that time. In most cases, there are three categories of lost souls:

1. Those who do not believe that they are dead. These are the ones whose death was sudden and/or traumatic. When that bright light appears, they cannot understand that it is for them. They are in disbelief. Sometimes they wait too long, and it becomes increasingly difficult to find.

2. Those who have unfinished business. These are the spirits who think that they must take care of their families or pets. Sometimes it can be a lifetime of work that they feel they need to protect. It is nearly

impossible to correct anything you did on earth once you have crossed over.

3. Those who do not believe that they deserve to go into the light. These are the ones who think that they have done something so heinous in this life that what waits for them on the other side of the light is judgment and damnation. These people have decided that to live in limbo as a spirit who has not crossed is the best choice that they can make. There is a lot more that can be said about this topic.

Once a friend asked me to check on someone who had committed suicide. For many who have taken their own lives, the period after death can be very confusing. Many I have met are lost, and many deny that they are dead and have created an alternate reality to explain why they are there. In this case, every time I tried to find him, he would seem to evade me by changing the wigs that he was wearing. He avoided even having a conversation with me.

While I could confirm to my friend that he had not crossed over, I had difficulty understanding the ever-changing wigs' significance. It was not until she told me that he had shot himself in the head that I understood. He covered what he had done and did not accept the reality of his situation.

I went back several times to find him. The last time, I asked for the assistance of my guides. This time we were able to talk with him. First, we sat him down in a room and made him take off the wigs that he had been using to hide his wounds from himself. We made him acknowledge that he was dead, which he eventually did. He was still reluctant to pass into the light, as that would be giving up on the illusion that he was still alive. Several other guides came in and surrounded him with golden light, and assisted him in moving toward the light. I got the impression that he needed to walk to the light himself. We got to the portal. Jessica was there holding it open and let him look in. It was at that point he decided that he was ready, and finally crossed over.

Eventually, I had one experience that I have never been able to relay to others without tears. While meditating one day, I felt a female spirit in my room. I asked her for her name. She told me that her real name was Diana, but people called her DeeDee. I said, "Hi, DeeDee."

I then asked her a question that I started to ask everyone who came to me: what year they think it is. Generally, they will tell me the year they died, since time stops for them. She said that it was 1974. I was taken aback by that and then asked how old she was. She told me, "14."

I said, "Oh, honey, what have you been doing for so long?"

As a parent of two teenage girls at that time, her response broke my heart. She said that she was looking for her mom and dad. She just wanted to let them know that she was okay. I told her that I did not know if I could help her find her parents, but I could take her to a place where her grandparents were and that her parents would eventually end up there if they were not there already. I asked if she would like to go. She agreed.

Jessica went toward the door as she always does, but before she could get to it, it opened slightly from behind and a man and a woman dressed in white came through. As they did, DeeDee started running and crying out, "Mommy! Daddy!" They embraced for a long time and then walked arm in arm into the light as Jessica proudly held the door for them.

Jessica and I were doing important work together, but I wanted to deepen my understanding of our history. Learning about our shared past lives became a profound healing experience.

Chapter 9

Visiting Jessica in Other Lifetimes

"I have always loved you"

A s I thought about writing about this book, I wanted to understand if Jessica and I had shared some past lives and if anything of significance happened in those lives. Luckily, I have a very dear friend and teacher, Jacki, who could help me with that.

Several weeks later, I reclined in her office as she hypnotized me to take me on a journey. As I went into a trance, I felt paralyzed. My body could not move. Lying on my back, at one point I felt strange, as though my legs were crossed. I knew that I did not want to cut off the circulation so I fought to see if I could uncross them, only to find out that they were not crossed. The only other time I felt a similar sensation was when I had a nerve block during knee surgery. From that point forward, I completely surrendered to the experience.

Eventually, in meditation Jacki presented me with three doors into other lives, but at that time, she also set an intention that in the spirit world, there is no past, present, or future. Time does not exist. Some future or current events could appear just as easily as lives from hundreds or thousands of years ago, but all events would be significant in helping me understand my relationship with Jessica at a deeper level.

The Village Square

I entered the first door as the fog cleared. I found myself in a large field. Around me, I saw an expansive meadow with several large trees near me. They looked like fruit trees. In the distance, I saw a castle. Jacki instructed me to look at what I was wearing. I looked down and saw that I was wearing a tunic with sandals on my feet. I appeared to be in the Middle Ages. When asked if I lived in the castle, I said, "no."

Jacki then instructed me to go to a place where Jessica might be. I moved to the village square. I saw a beautiful young lady across the square and felt an immediate connection. When asked if I talked to her, I said no. The next question was, "Would you like to?"

For some reason, I said no to that too. In that life, I died a content man with my wife and three daughters surrounding my deathbed. I think what I learned is that even though we had a spiritual connection, there may have been many lifetimes that we were not together, as we each understood that the life lessons were much more important than sharing a life. I still do not fully understand why I was shown that scene other than to say that at times, what we each needed to learn in that existence did not involve connecting.

Jacki then took me out to where the three doors had been. Only now, there were just two. The door that I had entered was gone and replaced with a mural of the village square that I had just visited. Next, I was instructed to go through the middle door.

Jitara

I went ahead through the door and after passing into another lifetime, I found myself standing alone, wearing a dark orange, almost red Buddhist monk's robe. I felt as though I was about twelve years old and somewhere in northern India. There was a chill in the air, and I shivered as I only wore a thin robe and had a clean-shaven head. I saw a market across from me, and in front of it, a young female street merchant was grilling up food on short carved sticks like shish kebabs. We seemed to be about the same age. Suddenly, I heard her call out in a loud voice, "BUN-DELÉ!" That must have been my name. "Bundelé, come here quickly! I have some delicious food for you."

As with any outdoor market, the air was filled with a strange mixture of spices, fresh vegetables, animals, raw meat, and all kinds of foods being cooked over fires by various street vendors simultaneously. I walked over to her and she noticed me shivering, took the scarf off her head, and wrapped it around my shoulders. She pushed me closer to the fire over which she was cooking so that I could warm up. The vegetables that she had just grilled tasted so delicious that they almost melted in my mouth. I did not realize just how hungry I had felt before that moment. Even though I was a monk, I still felt a strong affection for this girl, much like any teenage boy has for a pretty teenage girl. I guess monks have hormones too.

Her name was Jitara. Coming from a poor family, her parents expected her to aid the family from an incredibly early age. She never thought of her work as a burden, only as an obligation of being born into that life at that time. She never seemed depressed or sad because of her lot in life; it was just the way it was. Despite her meager life, she always brought a ray of sunshine into the lives of those she met, especially to this young monk. I seemed very smitten with her.

A few years later, I saw myself wandering around that village but always ending up in that same marketplace, sometimes sitting off in the distance just watching Jitara. Most of the time, I would get caught staring and would get called over to partake in some tasty food. I continued to watch the story of that girl play out, as seen through Bundelé's eyes.

One day Jitara, in tears, told me that she must marry a man that her parents selected for her. I, too, got tears in my eyes when I realized that our fates were never to be together. My parents chose mine when they left me orphaned at the temple as an infant, and hers was set when her mother and father picked her husband. As with most in that part of the world, the children did not have much choice with the direction of their lives.

I was invited to attend her wedding along with other monks from the local temple. The weather that day was perfect. As I watched the ceremony, it felt as though my heart was being ripped out of my body, but I stood there as if it were just like any other wedding I had attended. I even smiled at one point, but in my soul, the rain fell. Each time I looked at her, the pain seemed to intensify. In my mind, I knew that this day would happen, but it did not ease the pain of a young monk's broken heart. The question of how I could go on knowing that she belonged to someone else pounded in my head.

About a year later, after Jitara had her first child, she brought him to the temple to be blessed. She was such a proud mother; I could see that she loved her newborn son so much. When I first saw her there, I had butterflies in my stomach, as I was both excited and nervous to see her. She was still as beautiful as ever. This time, I could see an extra glow that comes with motherhood. She looked so content. I was, at that moment, happy for her. We may not be together, but at least I could have the comfort of knowing that she was happy in her new role.

Over the years, she had several more children, but each time she returned to the temple to have those babies blessed, I saw the happiness that was once such a huge part of her personality slowly disappearing. Life had taken its toll. As her children got older, she began to come to the temple alone more often to pray for them. On one of those trips, I noticed the bruising on her arms and face. When I asked her about it, she dismissed it as being nothing. Inside, the rage grew, but also the realization and frustration that there was nothing that I could do. My role was to not intervene in those circumstances, as each person must be allowed to live out their fate.

Time passed, and the Monk Bundelé became known throughout the region for his wisdom. Years of meditation, prayers, and prostrations had polished the once rough-cut monk into a gem of knowledge and understanding about the ways of life and the Buddha. People would come from far away to have an audience with me, but no matter how busy I became, I would always be available for Jitara. She eventually confessed to being abused by her husband. Given the time and location, there was not much that I could do except comfort her. Each time after she left, I would have to retreat to my private room where I would weep, sometimes for hours on end. The love that I felt would not die, no matter the roles that each of us had to play.

We both got older. Jitara's husband passed on to his next life. Life had been difficult for her, but at least she had her children to take care of her. Over time it became increasingly difficult for her to visit the temple as often as she wanted. Her children and then her grandchildren would have to help her because she was so determined to go. Eventually, her body weakened to the point that she stopped coming altogether.

One day, while I held an audience with a small group who had come to visit, a young monk approached and whispered in my ear. I immediately excused myself and found my way to Jitara's home. When I arrived, all her children and grandchildren surrounded her bed. Her eldest son stepped away and asked if he could talk to me for a moment. He told me that his mother's time left on earth was limited, but her last request was to see the monk called Bundelé one more time.

As the son and I moved forward to Jitara's bed, I was extremely nervous, not knowing what I would see. It had been so long since I had seen her. Even though time had taken its toll, in this monk's eyes, she looked as beautiful as that young girl in the market so many years ago. She glanced up, and when she saw me, a slight smile came to her lips. She reached out her hand to me. Without thinking, I grabbed it, and for the first and last time, we held hands. She pulled me closer and spoke in my ear; her voice was so weak that I could hardly hear her, but in a breathy, almost inaudible voice, she said, "I have always loved you."

I whispered back, "And I, you."

With that, she let out her last breath, her spirit left the body, and she began her journey to the spirit realm. I wept privately for days.

I lived for several more years. And during that time, I continued to provide counseling and spiritual advice to those who had journeyed to visit. Strangely, much like today, I could feel Jitara's presence with me often. Sometimes during my audiences, she would sit next to me, whispering in my ear and helping give guidance to those in attendance. Other times she came through as an overwhelming feeling of love. I liked those occasions the best, each time feeling increasingly connected and loved.

As my death grew nearer, the veil between life and death thinned. As I began my journey to the world of spirits, the first face I saw was hers. In my mind, I heard her sweet voice say, "At last, we are now together again." And we journeyed into the light together.

The Spirit World

My view into that life ended, and once again, I was back to where the three doors had been. The second door had been replaced by a mural of the scarf that Jitara had given to Bundelé on that chilly night. What a perfect symbol of Jitara's love.

Now it was time for the final door. When the fog cleared, I seemed to be in a different dimension. I felt as though I was nowhere and everywhere at the same time. I looked at my body and did not see one. What I saw was more like an energy field. I do not know if I had arms or legs, as there was only energy.

I looked around. I wanted to see where I was. I initially did not understand what I was experiencing, but I realized that I might be in the spirit realm. Off in the distance, I saw what seemed to be other energy forces flowing as they moved about their business. Suddenly, I felt a whoosh. I had a sensation of two energies melding together as one.

We were separate beings, but somehow the spirit felt as one soul, just how I imagined it felt before the initial separation. The one that I had traveled so far and so many lifetimes to see had just arrived. I knew that feeling immediately. It belonged to my beloved Jessica. Somehow, I felt as though she embraced me and kissed me. The kiss felt like a vibration on my lips. She seemed to be in a hurry, as she must have known that she had so much to say to me with minimal time.

We moved off to a secluded location. I am not sure how, but it felt as though we flowed there more than walked. We began to talk. Words seemed to be downloaded into my head. The priority was to explain the purpose and reasons behind her most recent lives.

She told me that it was vital that as I tell the story of us, people understand what happened in her two most recent lives, as there can be misconceptions about those whom we meet during our lifetime. She explained that during my one lifetime, she had two lifetimes that she experienced. She began to explain how soul contracts played a significant part in her last two incarnations.

Free of karmic debt, Jessica did not have to incarnate in either life, but did so to help others with their paths. When we think of a heavenly spirit coming to help others, we may think of a counselor, coach, or angel, but her contributions were not as simple as that. She had commitments or contracts with others to help them learn the lessons they needed by creating hardships.

As we make life plans for each incarnation to learn the things that we want and need, we work with other spirits and guides to create outcomes that will help us learn. For instance, suppose you were a wealthy and influential person in one of your previous lives but may have wanted to work on humility. In that case, you may plan that your next life is one of poverty and subservience to others. We set up contracts or commitments with other spirits and our guides to help us learn those lessons.

This process is all complicated because at birth, and as we get socialized into our lives, this information gets lost or forgotten, but it is always there just like a seed. Most end up feeling and crawling their way through their lives and have varying degrees of success. We all have lessons that we need to learn. Many times, it can take several attempts to release even one aspect of our karmic debt.

In the first of her two most recent lifetimes, she lived in a small farming community in Japan. As a child, she worked hard to help her family as much as possible, but she could just as easily be found at other farmers' homes peppering them with questions from an early age. She would ask things like, "How do you tell the chicken how many eggs to lay in one day?" Or "Why do some eggs have two yokes instead of one?"

Every time she went to their farms, it brought joy into their sometimes-mundane lives, especially for the older farmers whose children had already grown up. Her parents struggled at times to provide for the family, but loved her very much. No matter the hardship, they always found the money necessary to pay for education. It always came first in the budget. At 12 years old, she entered middle school. That meant she got to wear the official school uniform. For each student from that era, it was a status symbol. In their young minds, that was when they officially became one of the older kids, and with that came the expectation of respect.

Each school day, she proudly donned her white blouse and black skirt school uniform and made her way to school along a narrow dirt road. She had such a vibrant personality, and everyone enjoyed seeing her bounce down the road as she skipped along the way. The other farmers working in their fields would often look up as she passed, smile, and wave to her. She would always return the wave and continue skipping her way to school. She loved everything about school: the teachers, the homework, and even when she had to clean the dusty chalkboards or mop the floor on her hands and knees with a wet towel.

Just after her 13th birthday, one evening a little after dusk as she and some friends were returning from school, they heard a vehicle coming down the road. As per usual, they moved as far to one side of the road as they could without stepping into a water-soaked and muddy rice paddy, and stopped to wait for the vehicle to pass. A young local farmer was driving that small truck and took his eyes from the road to glance down at something that had fallen on the vehicle's floorboard. The road was narrow, and he veered ever so slightly.

He did not even see her when he felt and heard that sickening thud followed by the thump of his tire running over something. Initially, he hoped that he had hit some unseen debris. It was not until he heard the other girls' screams that he realized that something must be terribly wrong.

He jumped out of his truck and saw the young student surrounded by her friends, lying in a pool of blood. He reached down to see if there appeared to be any sign of life, but there was none. She had died instantly. He fell to his knees and sobbed uncontrollably while the other students ran to get help.

The young farmer's life changed instantly. How could he show his face again, especially to the parents of the girl? The farmer had to pay compensation to the family of the deceased girl. He became reclusive, turned to alcohol, and spent months enveloped in despair, depression, and self-loathing. That death devastated the community. How could they honor the life of the girl without disowning this once valued member of the community? They knew it was an accident, but a vibrant young life had ended. That death tore apart the village, as it was one of their own that had hit and killed this amazing young girl.

Over the next few years, as the community agonized about the nature of that death, they ever so slowly began to come together in love and forgiveness. During this time, the young farmer's life also changed, as he moved from a self-destructive course to a selfless path that he is still on today. He entered a Buddhist monastery, where he spent months in deep, intense soul-searching meditation, became clean from unhealthy addictions, and went on to impact and change the lives of many with whom he has come in contact.

As we can see many times in life, people who have experienced the most unimaginable circumstances are the same ones who turn that experience into a starting point for bringing change, and as they heal from their pain, they help many others heal in the process.

Jessica's most recent life was a little more complicated, and full of many things that may look different on the outside from what they really were. When I first discovered Jessica and tried to learn of her most recent life, it bothered me that she did not have this perfect Mother Teresa-type life, or even one in which I would have been involved had our paths ever intersected. If I wanted to create this wonderful story of meeting my soul twin, I would not have sought her out.

When I found mugshots online from arrests related to drugs and alcohol, it painted her in less than perfect light, and it left me with such an unsettled feeling. How could this person with whom I felt such powerful spiritual experiences have had such a troubled life? I had spent most of my life trying to create this wonderful fiction around who I was. Now that I was trying to piece together the most important story that I will ever share, how could I tell others that this spirit with whom I have this amazing connection was not a perfect person who lived a long, saintly life of service to others? That did not fit the façade of the Bruce that I wanted to portray.

Jessica's most recent life was far from the story that I wanted to tell, one that was free of visible defects. But through writing this, I have come to realize that no one lives an idealized life. No one comes out of each life without the scars that make them who they are, and we should not look upon those as defects, but as medals of honor. It is not the unrealistically perfect life that makes each of us, but the hardships.

I have found that when I felt troubled with the life that she lived, I only saw that life in a vacuum. I was only looking at it through the lens of how I would tell this story, and by doing so, how the story of her life would reflect on me. That blinded me to the entirety of her beautiful soul and the service that she was performing.

Jessica filled those around her with love. Fiercely loyal to those in her inner circle, they knew that she loved them. After her death, one of her friends commented that he hoped her face was the first thing he saw immediately upon his death. Another said that her advice seemed to come from the heart and was always accurate. Those who knew her best did not doubt the level of her caring and concern. From all accounts, she was extremely artistic and creative.

However, she had her challenges. Somehow, she seemed to sense the nobility of her soul and would become frustrated with circumstances, and the confinement that she felt on earth did not match the majesty of her soul's purpose. This impression and life were by design. At a subconscious level, she struggled with the feeling that she should have been destined for a higher calling, but instead was restricted to her mortal body and the life she had chosen here on earth. The internal conflicts, self-doubts, and pain would lead to addictions that would eventually bring about her early death.

She did bring two amazing children into this world who had significant plans for their lives here. Her face lit up when she talked about them; they were her two awesome treasures. She still loves them dearly.

They had all worked together before her birth to create their life designs. A significant portion of those plans required them to have a mother who, even though she deeply loved them, had the kind of challenges that Jessica faced. Despite having an incredibly caring and supportive father and extended family support system, these children would lose their mother early in life. Jessica's children have important life plans; had they not had early childhood experiences and lost their mother when they were young, they would not have the tools to later achieve those plans.

In life, the greatest successes often come from the most significant losses. This pattern seems to be a universal truth. For a person to produce remarkable things, there must be obstacles to overcome.

In a traditional sense, many religions teach that we come to earth to prove ourselves worthy of going back into heaven. Those who do good works and follow the rules prescribed on this earth will go there, but those who do not will be thrown into a lake of fire and brimstones where they are always burning but never consumed.

What if it does not work that way? What if some of the most troubled humans are higher-level souls that have volunteered to serve by helping others fulfill their soul contracts? It would be easy to create black-and-white terms to live our lives by, but we all know that real life is more nuanced and with varying shades of grey.

Jessica did not have to come back to earth; she did so to help others learn what they needed to progress. That is the beauty of her sacrifice and the service that she performed.

After learning about that, I came to love her even more. As the Bible says: "There is no greater love than to lay down one's life for one's friends."

Her two most recent lives were all about love.

The Nature of Love

Near the end of my session with Jacki, she encouraged me to ask Jessica about her life specialties or even my own. I told her with an almost immediate understanding that Jessica's soul's specialty has always been about unconditional love. This is not about giving and receiving love; it is much deeper than that. She *is* love, the very embodiment of that energy. It is so fundamental to her soul that no matter the incarnation, I am almost certain that it was clear to those around her.

I have felt and seen her energy in the brief time since she has come back into my life. Sometimes it manifests in subtle ways, like a vibration in the palm of my hand, a line from a song, or the voice that tells me to get up and keep moving forward. At other times it is an all-encompassing feeling of being unconditionally loved. Throughout her soul's journey, that has always been clear.

When I asked what she wanted for me or what I need, she said one thing that I must learn on this earth is that love is not external. Every person *is* love. It comes from within. It is not a feeling or emotion; it just is. Love is so core and fundamental but often the most challenging element to realize. It comes from the very essence of each of us. When I understand that, I will be close to understanding this life's purpose.

Jessica said that any gifts or talents that I may have are not as crucial as developing that love and understanding of just who I am. Any gifts that I do have are like tools on the belt. Those are not as necessary as love, but merely manifestations of it. Her hope for me is to better understand this and have the confidence to share that love with others through all my actions. That is the most meaningful change I could make in my life, to get me closer to where I need to be.

Several months after that experience, one Sunday, I began to get a sense of this. I was meditating, and something quite different happened. I felt somehow that I connected to an enlightened being in another dimension. The connection just seemed different than anything that I can remember. I thought that I should not let this opportunity pass without asking some questions, on the chance that I really was in touch.

For some reason, I felt extremely interested in learning if I could connect to Source directly, and what that would mean for me. As I was having a conversation with this being, I asked, "If I could, how would I contact Source? Does it have a name?"

The being chuckled and asked me, "Can you name every atom on earth? That is kind of like what you are asking." It went on to explain that everything is a part of Source. Then, the being used Donald Trump as an example, knowing that I am not a huge fan of the man, and said, "You are part of him, just as he is part of you, and both are part of Source."

Something happened to me when I heard those words. For the first time in my life, I felt an intense love for Trump.

Would I want to hang out with him, or would I vote for him? The answer is clearly, "No!" Do I feel a love for him? Yes! Why? He is part of me and part of Source. How could I not love something that is part of me?

This feeling and the bond I felt were very strong, and I began to see others on this earth: criminals, neighbors, co-workers, newborn babies, and a battlefield doctor covered in blood as she was trying to save a recent victim of a bombing. I felt that deep love and compassion for all of them. I realized that we are everyone, and everyone is us. I felt so connected to humanity and the energy of all on this earth in a way that I never have before. My very existence depended on everyone else's. For that moment, there was no separation.

That feeling of connection to everyone and everything has changed my perception of this thing called life. It is one thing intellectually to understand the concept, but quite another to viscerally *feel* that interrelatedness.

I know that I am just beginning to understand the Oneness, but I want more if it is anything like I experienced that day. Maybe, it is just the kind of love that Jessica wants me to learn about, a true love that does not require any external input. It just is.

Imagine if we could all experience that kind of love and then understand that we rely on each other for our very existence. We are all a part of the universe's Source energy. How different would our choices be, and how would we treat others, if we truly knew this?

Chapter 10

Visiting Her Grave

"The part of me that is part of you"

A year into our relationship, I began planning to visit Jessica's grave. I found my window of opportunity when I realized that I could attend a football game, visit with my daughter, and make a quick trip to the cemetery all in the same weekend. I felt a bit conflicted about it though. Going to visit the "final resting place" of someone who was very much alive seemed strange to me. But I wanted to pay my respects to the body that once clothed her soul.

Every life impacts others; sometimes, it is like a stone's ripple effect after being tossed in a calm lake. Other times it can be like a giant wave crashing upon those with whom they come in contact. Each soul whose body is lying in that place deserves to be recognized for their struggles and their influence on others while incarnated.

That day, I was there to recognize the mortal life of one of those in the cemetery, not only for the impact she'd had on those around her when she was living, but for how she had completely changed my life after she left that body.

I had already prepared a note to place on the grave well in advance. I think that I wanted those who may read it to understand that Jessica's influence went much further than they might have known. If I were to be honest, beyond the note I was hoping that I could actually run into someone there who knew Jessica. I really wanted to tell them the amazing story of the Jessica that I had come to know, and let them know that she is alive and happy.

I stopped at a store on my way to the cemetery to buy some flowers. I initially selected a beautiful bouquet, but at the last minute, I switched as I saw one with more vivid colors, wrapped in purple tissue. I had no idea then, but I found out later that purple was her favorite color.

Because music has always been so crucial to how she has communicated with me, I wondered what her choice would be as I drove up to her grave. After I left the store and began the short drive to the grave, the entertainment system played "Lovely Day" by Bill Withers, which seemed appropriate as the sun was indeed shining in my eyes. I smiled, but as I turned into the cemetery, the song changed. It was not something that I knew, and I was initially a little disappointed because I had spent much of the trip wondering which song she would pick for that moment as I drove up to her grave.

When I found Jessica's grave, I was extremely impressed with the stone that marked her site. The stone did not appear in Google's Street view, so I had not seen it in my research. It was a beautiful granite headstone. I felt thrilled that someone had cared enough to place the marker on her grave. It showed the love of those she left behind. As I stood there thinking about the last year of my life and what a fantastic experience that it had been, I felt remorse for those who had to lose so much for me to gain.

Suddenly, that vibration that I had felt nearly a year prior came back, along with the intense feeling of being unconditionally loved. Tears, again, came to my eyes as I stood there, feeling her loving presence. I knew that she appreciated my effort to pay my respects to that life.

I took some final photos of her headstone and left. I began to listen to the song that was playing when I entered the cemetery. The song was Ben Platt's "In Case You Don't Live Forever." The song calls out the idea of "the part of me that is part of you." What a wonderful way to describe a twin flame. She had picked the perfect song as I drove toward her grave after all. I listened to it repeatedly as I drove back to Boise, crying tears of love each time.

After that experience, something changed. I felt so much more connected to Jessica, and very synchronistic events began to happen. It began that night as I tried to sleep. I got the urge to tell some people who knew my story about my road trip that day. I posted a photo of Jessica's gravestone with a summary of my experience of the day and shared it with a select group of friends on Facebook.

Catherine commented and asked if I had ever considered writing a book about my experience. I wrote back that I had not, but immediately the title *Finding Jessica* came to mind. I later found out that that title was already taken, so I eventually changed it to the current title. I also thought that everyone seemed to be writing books these days. If I did write one, it would most likely be lost in a pile of other unread books from other well-intentioned authors.

If I had received only one comment, I might not have decided to pursue it, but something magical happened later.

The following Saturday, I attended an all-day spiritual workshop. The event was held in an old Baptist church in the Capitol Hill area of Seattle. This place is one of the oldest church buildings in the city and not a typical location for this kind of seminar, as the day's curriculum would not be close to a normal Baptist one. The weather seemed unusually chilly even for the Pacific Northwest in late September. I arrived a little early to get a good seat, but had to wait outside on a wide flight of granite steps flanked by handrails until the doors opened.

As I stood waiting to enter, I noticed a woman standing in line across from me talking with two of her friends. I did a double take; I was shocked by what I saw. Her brunette hair with a reddish tint, parted on the right and cut just at the shoulders with the bottom slightly curving towards the front, her nose, and her eyes were remarkably similar to the many photographs I had seen of Jessica.

I could not believe it. I knew that it was not her, but it felt like she was standing across from me in the queue. In disbelief, I tried to sneak glances at her. I could not comprehend what was happening, but I knew that I did not want to be caught staring at some random married woman in line.

The doors opened, and in the lobby, there were tables set up for the check-in process. After verifying my name and receiving a wristband, I moved into the chapel to look for the best seat to grab for the day. I sat in the second row just to the right of where the teacher would be. After I sat down, I looked around at all the others who had taken their places. I was particularly interested in where the Jessica look-alike would sit. I just felt drawn to her for some reason; maybe it was nothing more than a desire to feel a better connection with Jessica.

To my surprise, she sat directly behind me. What are the odds of that? At the beginning of the day, I would have said that they were long. By the end, I would have told you the opposite. I wanted to speak with her, but what would I say? "Hi, you look just like the photos of a dead woman I have seen online." That would take a creepy stalker vibe to a whole new level. It was probably not the best way to begin a conversation with someone. My best hope was to have some interaction as part of the activities of the workshop.

If you have ever been to one of these events, you may know how high the energy can be. There was no exception in the chapel that day, and it created a great learning environment. In one of the first activities, we worked with a partner to feel the other person's energy and assess if the other one had any energy blockages. As we found blockages, we were instructed to attempt to clear them energetically.

I partnered with an older woman who sat across the aisle from me. I discovered that this woman had raised thirty-two children throughout her life, many with special needs. Other than that, I knew nothing about her, as we had just met. She scanned my body first and discovered, no surprise to me, that I had energy blockages in my throat area that prevented me from speaking my truth.

Then it was my turn to scan her. When I did, I felt a large amount of energy streaming from the heart and a tremendous amount flowing from the top of her head. She seemed very connected. I also felt an enormous weight on her shoulders. She confirmed that and said that she felt burdened by the sheer enormity of her responsibilities as a mother, wife, and caregiver for many years. She said that she still carried that around, but now that she was retired, it was time to let go.

At this point, she stopped our conversation and looked me straight in the eye, and asked if I had ever thought about authoring a book. She continued and said that while I was scanning her, she had this overwhelming impression that I had a book in me that needed to be written, and this book was particularly important. I was speechless, but many questions fired off in my head in the seconds following that comment.

Ten minutes prior, I did not know this woman, and she knew nothing about me, my life, or what Catherine had said to me a few days earlier. How could she even know that? I was stunned. Tears welled up in my eyes. I had a Jessica look-a-like sitting behind me, and now I was once again being asked about a book. These people had obviously never spoken to any of my former English teachers, because if they had, they would not have been asking such a ridiculous thing.

As I wrote to Catherine during a lunch break, I thought that the universe was slapping me in the face telling me to write the book. She answered back and said that it sounded like a pretty deafening scream. The universe, or rather Jessica, was not done yet.

At the end of the day, I was finally paired with the woman who sat behind me, the Jessica look-alike. Of all things, we did a mediumship exercise in which the person acting as the medium attempts to connect with the other person's loved one. Because most of the participants were inexperienced at this, the person receiving the reading was to give three details about the loved one they would like to hear from: a name, the type of relationship, and a personality trait.

I went first. Usually, I would have said my mother, father, or even my Aunt Mary. On that day, as I was gazing at a woman that looked just like her, I decided to go for it. I did not want to waste this opportunity. I said, "Jessica, friend, loving presence."

At once, this woman seemed to connect with Jessica. She said that Jessica told her that I had recently changed the path I was on and that she was so happy about it. She indicated that Jessica was always with me, often whispering in my ear. She did not miss anything. How bizarre was this whole situation? There I sat, listening to this woman who looked like Jessica telling me what Jessica was saying to her.

Then she indicated that Jessica showed her what seemed to be an ancient scroll tied carefully with a ribbon. She undid the ribbon to reveal an exceedingly long, immaculately hand-written text and indicated that she wanted me to continue writing the story. The impression I got was that Jessica had been recording our story until then, and now it was my turn to continue the process.

To say that I felt overwhelmed with emotion would be an understatement. What a beautiful visual representation of the ancient history that we have shared together, and how it was now my responsibility to continue the recording. I now had Jessica telling me that I needed to write this book. Three times within one week, I had been told to write a book by three different women. Any choice I thought I had in the matter suddenly evaporated. I knew that I had to write.

Later, I connected with the grandfather of this woman, and at the end of this session, I received a special unexpected treat. Even though we did not know each other, we felt a strong connection, and we gave each other a big hug.

For the briefest moment, it actually felt as if I was holding Jessica for the first time in this lifetime. I did not want to let go. It felt like my only physical connection to her. The act of embracing another person is such a beautiful human experience and something that I had never experienced with Jessica in this life. What a blessing that I could experience that for a moment.

As we said good-bye, I had to fight back the emotions and tears. I then knew why I was so strangely drawn to this woman from the moment I saw her that morning. Jessica was working through this amazingly connected soul to convey a very important message to me.

The message was clear. Jessica loved me. I needed to write this book, and she would be there to help.

Chapter 11

Finally Cutting the Ties

A powerful healing

I've mentioned the profound impact my parents' decision to leave me with a neighbor shortly after my birth had on my life, and how I constantly felt the need to defer to power growing up. Though it's easy to dismiss the experience as having been such a short amount of time at such a young age, much scholarly research has been done on the subject of early attachment, and based on my own experience, I have found it to be true. "Cutting the ties that bind" is a method by which one can energetically disconnect the ties to a difficult or traumatic experience or person.

This process had begun in Catherine's office almost a year and a half prior. The connection was hindering my further spiritual development. Just writing this makes me think about how strange that may sound, but it was indeed an energetic connection: the connection to feeling abandoned at birth. It does not matter how far away from that birth imprint we are; we are still affected by it.

I began to work with Michael again when the theme of my dreams began to change, and I felt I needed a deeper understanding and exploration. Based on the dreams he had interpreted in my first session; it became evident that I still had not completely severed those traumatic energetic ties around the feeling of abandonment.

The "cutting ties" method involves creating a daily "plus and minus" list of the person from whom you are trying to disconnect energetically, and doing a prescribed energetic exercise. During this time, Michael watched my dreams. I can say that some of the most unique dreams that I have ever had appeared during this time. Also, my emotions move from depression to anger for seemingly no reason at all. I was more emotionally fragile at this time than I wanted to admit. Luckily for me, after three weeks, Michael noticed that my dreams had changed.

This was the dream that indicated I was finally ready to complete the process:

> I am in a basketball game. Former President Jimmy Carter is participating too. There is a struggle for the ball around the middle of the court. Suddenly, Jimmy takes two pink roses and throws them at the basket in what I assume is some symbolic gesture, but the roses go straight up over the top of him and fall to the ground, getting nowhere near the basket. I think that

this man has lived a life of service, and we can do better to honor his gesture. I pick up the roses and hand them back to him. Then I clear the crowd of players from around the basket and allow him to throw his two roses into the basket from close range, which he does.

Creating a path for the former president to complete the task indicated that I was ready to complete the process. Michael sent me a note that I needed to find a quiet place, as that day we would finish the process. It was time for me to cut the ties completely. I scheduled a quiet conference room where I knew that I would not be disturbed, and blocked my calendar for thirty minutes of distance healing with Michael.

When he began, I could see where I was symbolically and energetically connected to my mother. Three connections still existed and needed to be removed: the first was umbilical (leaving the womb), the second was the heart (leaving Jessica), and the final was my right leg (my ability to move on).

After removing the energetic connections, Michael instructed me in meditation to move into a river that appeared next to me and cleanse my body from any residual energy that remained. When this process was completed, I came out of the cleansing water and walked to the other side. He told me that my guides would be there waiting for me. As I walked from the water, they gave me a beautiful white robe with gold trim to wear. My guides stood smiling on the bank above me, but the way they were smiling reminded me of the way "Shoeless" Joe Jackson was smiling at Ray Cancesca in *Field of Dreams* just before he introduced Ray's father to him.

Suddenly from behind, I felt Jessica's arms come around me in a loving embrace. I felt that deep connection to her once again. A sense of euphoria swept through me. She seemed to whisper in my ear, "I am so proud of you. One more aspect of your karma has now been resolved."

A strong sense of complete joy and love overwhelmed me. Again, Jessica and I were reunited. Once more, our time together seemed too brief, but the impact I still feel today. She had appeared again, just when I needed her. I often wonder how many times she has been there for me throughout our many lives.

Chapter 12

Creative Ways of Communicating

Our secret language

When two people are on opposite sides of the veil, it allows opportunities to learn about how to converse. Communication can be difficult enough in earthly relationships when everyone is on the same plane of existence; just imagine the complexity of communicating across time dimensions and frequencies.

Music

Music can be magical. The melodies alone can make your spirit soar or take you to the depths of sorrow. When you add lyrics, it can make the songs even more effective at sending messages or conveying an emotion. It may leave your heart singing, comfort a broken heart, or bring peace of mind.

From the beginning, Jessica would drop songs on me. From the first song, "I Honestly Love You," to "Jump," and many in between and after, Jessica has given me some amazing messages in the form of music. Music has always been an essential part of one of the creative ways she has communicated with me. Sending me particular songs not only conveys an emotion, feeling, or thought but also helps me understand that one of my spiritual gifts is that of clairaudience or hearing messages of the spirit.

I wish there was a way to share the exact lyrics and how each one personally affected me or helped me understand a different aspect of our relationship, but because of copyright restrictions, I am not able to do so at this time. I have, however, included a playlist of songs she has sent me in the Appendix at the end of this book.

She has employed so many different methods of providing me musical messages, and I started to place them in an ever-expanding playlist. Sometimes, I will wake up with a portion of a lyric, like "hold my hand," with a set of particular notes. That phrase appears in numerous songs, but it only appears in one when combined with that particular set of notes. Many days I have awakened from a dream with as little as three words and three notes. It makes for a really fun internet search game as I track down that song. And I am always amazed to find other hidden messages within that song once I find those exact lyrics.

Other times, it will be a song that I have never heard before, like something from a random playlist that I am listening to for the first time. Most of the time, they are reminders of the love that we share, or that she is watching over me. On other occasions, they can be a humorous jab at me for not progressing as fast as she thinks that I should, like in Pink's song, "True Love." Listen to the lyrics sometime, and you will understand.

What is it about music that can convey such powerful messages, and why would she choose that medium to communicate? I think that some of it involves pre-life planning. We planned on using music as a way to communicate during this time in my life. Some of it has brought chills, and at other times, left me weeping with a combination of sheer happiness and the utter despair of a kind of loneliness that I have up to that point in my life never felt.

Whatever it is, I would prefer having an in-person conversation, but there seems to be limits to that, so we must be creative.

Signs

During the coronavirus pandemic's initial days, many people, including me, had no idea of the impact or total disrup-
tion that this would have on everyone's lives worldwide. In
what was the blink of an eye, if and how we worked or performed even the simplest of tasks became a tricky question.

One day my daughter's college decided to move to online-
only classes to control the virus's spread. The next week
they decided to close the dormitories. I found myself making a round trip from Seattle to Boise, Idaho, to pick her up
from school. The day before, my good friends had helped
her move out of her dorm and put some of her stuff in
storage. Because at that time the state of Washington was
considered a high-risk area, and I had no idea if I had been
exposed to the virus, I arranged with my friends that I
would only stop long enough to pick up her and load her
stuff in the car.

It is a 15-hour round trip; I got up at 3 a.m. and was out
the door by 4. I downloaded *Signs: The Secret Language of
the Universe* on Audible to listen to on the way down. The
book is about looking and asking for signs from those on
the other side of the veil. As I was driving, I decided to ex-
periment and ask Jessica for a sign. I knew that her favorite
color was purple and asked her to show me something purple.

The sun was not out yet and it was still very dark. I passed through Yakima, Washington, and after a few miles, I saw something out of the corner of my eye. When I turned my head to look, I noticed a small building that was lit up with yellow and purple lighting, seemingly all by itself. I started to cry when I thought that was the sign. Just then, the author started to share a story about a purple balloon that had been a sign for someone.

Little did I know, Jessica was not done.

Later I passed a semi-truck with a purple cab. As soon as I passed it, the author started to talk about a four-digit sequence of numbers that appeared to someone, which was the birthdate of this person's son. It was also Jessica's birthday, a very clear sign. The following day I attended a Zoom call. One woman on the call kept talking about her favorite song being "Purple Rain." She must have said "Purple Rain" at least ten times. I thought of Jessica in the background laughing and asking, "Do I really need to show you more evidence at this point?"

Even though I know that she is a constant presence in my life, I guess that I am human and need to be reminded. If two people are physically present, it is very easy for them to indicate affection and love for each other, as they can easily see and talk with each other for validation. In our case, working across the veil, it is not so easy, so the signs and songs help considerably.

It was not until later that I figured out that I could channel her. When I discovered that, it made things much easier. It is not a perfect solution, but it does make me feel closer to her.

Chapter 13

Conversations with Her

It all came down to one simple concept, and that is love

Since this is a book about Jessica, someone suggested that I channel a conversation with her. I did not know how this would turn out, but I sat down with my computer one evening and just began typing questions. The answers started coming to me in ways that I did not expect. In the process, I gained insight into the purpose of life and the very nature of love. I present this in the order it happened.

First Discussion

Bruce: Thank you for agreeing to talk to me like this. Is it okay if I use your real name? As you know, up to this point, I have only referred to you as Jessica and Jitara. But your real (soul) name is Siseya, is that right?

Jessica: *Yes, it is.*

B: What name do you prefer?

J: *That is a great question. Because of where I am now, names are not that important, as we have different ways to communicate that do not involve words. Some of us who communicate with earthly beings still use names because that is how we can communicate with you. Most of the interactions are much like we have. You have come in contact with a lot of spirits recently, right? When I am with you, how do you know that it is me and not another spirit?*

B: It just feels different. You have a unique vibration, something that I can easily identify as you.

J: *When this happens, do I need to tell you who I am or announce my arrival?*

B: No.

J: *But you know that it is me?*

B: Yes, I do.

J: *That is remarkably similar to how we understand and know the people we are with or those with whom we would like to talk. Whereas you and I have this one-on-one connection, here in the spirit realm, it is possible to have that connection with all.*

B: That is fascinating. May I ask you some more questions?

J: *Of course, you are telling our story. The book would probably not be that good if you did not have more direct quotes from me. (She is giggling at this point)*

B: Good point.

J: *Do you remember when I showed Amanda the scroll?*

B: Amanda?

J: *That was the name of the woman who you thought looked like me at the seminar.*

B: Oh, yes.

J: *There was extra meaning to that scroll. Many things on that scroll have not been revealed to you because you are not ready. Yes, you are continuing the story, but there are so many beautiful truths written in that scroll that I would love to reveal to you when you are ready.*

B: So are you saying there is more to come?

J: *(Laughing again) If you only knew, or rather, could remember...*

B: So, on a scale of 1 to 100, how much do you think I know?

J: *I do not want to discourage you, so please understand when I tell you that your knowledge of the universe, while you are in your mortal body, is less than one percent. You have definitely seen glimpses, but a human mind has no way to comprehend the vastness or begin to understand the complexity.*

There are many things that I am learning now, much like when I was a little girl in Japan. I love everything about learning. That is one of the amazing things about being here; I am not limited to one class at a time. I can simultaneously be absorbing many topics at the same time. Occasionally, I teach classes, too, as each has their own unique area of expertise, and many want to learn. You would think that it would be very confusing to be teaching and learning simultaneously, but it is really awesome.

B: Talking to you like this is so cool. I wish that I had thought of it before.

J: *(Chuckling again) You weren't ready before. Please get some rest. We have much more to discuss.*

Second Discussion

B: Shall we continue our discussion?

J: *Of course.*

B: I have a lot of questions about the first time that you spoke to me after that dream. Do you think that we can discuss that?

J: *I will answer what I can.*

B: Great! When Jessica died, how long did it take for you to remember me?

J: *First of all, please remember that time is relative. As with all souls, no matter what kind of life you lived, once you enter the light, you are filled with so much loving essence that you are so at peace. I was greeted by people who I knew in that life that had gone before me. What was really strange is there were many spirits that I did not recognize, but there was something about them that I knew. For instance, your earthly parents were there. I knew them. I had no comprehension of why they were there. I later discovered that they are part of our soul family, and we have all been assisting each other through many lifetimes.*

After the welcoming party, I was taken to another area. It felt like a resort of sorts. It would help if you remembered that at this time, I was still Jessica. I did not remember Siseya. A soul's memory does not return immediately. There is a time

of healing and reflecting on the life that you have just com-
pleted. That is where I met the spirit who you knew as Kyle.

[Kyle is my nephew, who died many years ago in a skate-
boarding accident.]

Kyle was my counselor who took me through my life review.
He is such a kind and loving soul, and patiently guided me
through the process with many others' assistance, but he
seemed to take a special interest in my development. It was
not until I remembered you that I made the connection.

Everyone has trauma from their lives that they need to heal
from. My previous life was no exception. Even though I was
living it for others, I still was damaged in so many ways, but I
also learned so many great lessons. Moving through this, we
kept discussing the soul contract. At first, I thought that they
were crazy. I thought that I never signed up for anything in
that life, but the memories started to return little by little.

What I am about to tell you is very important, and I need
you to really understand what I am saying. During this entire
process, not once did I ever feel like I was being judged. I did
judge myself and questioned many decisions that I made, the
actions that I took, and the impacts those had on others, but
Kyle and my other counselors were only loving. I felt so sup-
ported throughout the whole process. There is no heaven or
hell, only different stages of acceptance around what you ex-
perienced in your life.

As my memory returned, I began to have glimpses of you. At
first, it was very hazy, almost like some sort of dream that I
knew I had, but could not remember any of the details about.

Slowly I remembered the details of you as a soul, but then I began to remember all of our past lives together. I find it interesting that some here never want to remember anything past their most recent life. At some point, they will have to, but they stubbornly cling to that life as if that is all that matters.

My memory grew to a point where suddenly, I had full recollection of everything. That moment felt like the entire universe came in alignment for me. Even though our paths, just like so many, have been extremely complex, it all came down to one simple concept, and that is love.

By the way, in English, there is just that one word that covers so many aspects. Here it is the opposite. We have many ways to express that concept of love. One of those is the love that powers the universe. That is what I experienced at that moment. I wish that I could give you that experience now, but that will have to wait. I get excited when I think about the day that you have the same experience, and we are together to share it. I will give you a hint. It is awesome! I have already experienced it, as there is no linear time here. I am just waiting for you to catch up.

Third Discussion

B: I know that even before you died this last time, some changes were going on in my life, but after your death is when things began to move quickly. Can you explain a little about what was happening that I could not see?

J: *Here is what you need to understand. Forces of angels and guides have worked and continue to work quietly and diligently in the background to set up situations and coincidences in your life to allow you the opportunity to select the path that you need to take. Do you think it was an accident that your department got moved into the same division where your friend who helped you begin your spiritual path worked before I died? You met her to begin to prepare yourself so that I could come back into your life. Or was it by chance that you met others after my death who have helped you on your path?*

These are not accidents. You are being connected to some of the strongest souls on earth. They were selected for you and countless others because of their connections to the Source. What is happening is quite remarkable, and there are reasons you are in this position. You and I will be part of the team that brings about these changes.

Fourth Discussion

B: May I ask about that night that you first spoke to me?

J: *I have been waiting for this question. Go ahead, what do you want to know?*

B: My first question is, how much involvement did you have in the dream the week before you first spoke to me? You know, the dream with the two girls on the train.

J: *We had that mapped out long before. Actually, you were the one that originally came up with the idea. It was all part of the pre-life planning, but as far as executing it, when someone's life matches with the plan, it almost becomes scripted. It is something that is planned and practiced before coming to earth. It is almost like an astronaut. Everything they do once the mission begins is very scripted, but that does not mean that there cannot be deviations should conditions change. Everyone has free will. Does that make sense?*

B: Yes, it does. Is the same true of the lake dream?

J: *Of course, the fun part for me was watching you squirm each time that dream repeated itself. (She is laughing) No, believe it or not, I was so anxious for the dream to end, too. It was the first time that I had a chance to speak to you again, but that also was scripted. What was funny is at the time, you thought that you were so spiritually connected, even though it had been only a few months. It was quite the trick to get my voice to travel down to you at the vibrational frequency you were at that time. That is why it may have sounded so strange to you. We used that to our advantage. It did make my voice very unique, right?*

B: Why didn't you give me any more information at that time?

J: *(Giggling again) Once again, that was the way we scripted it.*

B: I must ask about the Olivia Newton-John song. Did you choose that?

J: *That one was my choice. The song speaks of a woman who has discovered that she is in love with a man. Still, circumstances will not allow them to be together, but nonetheless, she knows that she must declare her love at that moment. That line also looks like it was directly pulled from the dream about the message coming from her heart and not her head. I loved that, and your reaction was precious.*

B: That seems so long ago, but also, I remember it like it was yesterday.

J: *Can we talk about love for a little bit?*

B: Absolutely, it is the main theme of the book.

J: *One thing that is unique about our situation is that we loved each other from the time we were created. The instant that our soul divided, the very essence was love. It was not something that we had to learn; it just existed. We shared that love while never depending on the other to fulfill it. Through that connection, we could fly higher, dream bigger, and accomplish more than if we were on our own, but the connection does not change the essence of the core of what love is. There is no codependency; it is only an enhancement.*

With each life, we have the opportunity to learn a new aspect of what that means. With each death, we have the chance to evaluate that and place it in the perspective of what it means. The cycle of life, death, and learning is such an amazing process. We have both had many lifetimes where our lessons came through neglect and abuse. Others where we felt the magic of love and feeling that deep soul connection while still in the human form. While the harsher lifetimes generally have greater growth benefits, I still cherish the lifetimes we have been together to experience that beautiful connection.

Fifth Discussion

B: It has been a while since I have spoken to you. Can we talk about my past/present life regressions that Jacki facilitated?

J: *I wish you could see all our former lives. The path that we have taken makes so much more sense when you can see everything. For me, each is beautiful, but like you, there is something about the Jitara story and the things we learned through the pain that is a perfect representation of what our love has been.*

As I said before, love is the essence of who we are, and it is eternal. We each function very well without each other, but together we become a powerful force. When I was working with our guides to determine which lives to present, it became clear that we needed to present the four that we did. Each one presented a different aspect of who we are. We could have shown only the ones where we lived together, but that does not create the portrait of what we have become.

B: This may be terrible to say, but my favorite part of the story of Bundelé and Jitara is the death bed scene when Jitara finally confesses what they both knew all along.

J: *I do like that. I am so happy that I said that because it was true at that moment and throughout eternity. I see you crying now. Your current body is susceptible to that, isn't it? (Smiles)*

I do love that you are that way for now. You cannot hide your emotions.

B: It is not very manly, is it?

J: *Yes, but in that, you really show your sensitive side.*

B: In the spontaneous past life regression about World War I, you played a psychopomp, and you are the one who taught me about helping the lost souls. How long have you been doing that?

J: *Let me just say that this is not "me" but "we." We have both been doing this from even before we originally separated. It has been an assignment that we have had. Sometimes, in our mortal states, either you or I will forget this, and we may have to be reminded.*

Please remember that this is a special gift and should always be treated with the utmost reverence and love. This process is all about helping souls go to the place where they need to be. It does not matter what kind of life the person may have lived. Each deserves to move into the light. Just like my two most recent lives, there are numerous factors that we may not understand about soul contracts. Our job is not to judge but to give all those a chance to cross over even if they are initially resistant.

Can you see that process is so critical to each soul's progression? Without that ending of the one life to eventually take on a new one, it's like running a race and never crossing the finish line. Most are just so afraid, and that is why we must treat them with so much love. It is an extremely holy act and must always be treated as such.

B: The moment that someone crosses over, I get such a high, it is almost like a state of euphoria. Can you explain that?

J: *(Smiling) Oh, that feeling. That is a soul-level feeling. What you are sensing is the excitement of those on the other side. In many cases, to use the finish line analogy, it is almost like when a marathon runner staggers across the line as they have depleted all of their energies just to get across the line.*

Think back to when you have witnessed this. While the winner of a race gets recognized for their accomplishment, many times, the biggest applause is for the athlete that has given their last ounce of energy just to cross the line. On this side of the veil, lost souls are treated much the same. Many wait for them just to cross over so that the healing can begin. When they arrive, a large burst of energy is released, like that of a cheering crowd.

Sixth Discussion

B: It has been a while since we have had a session.

(Note: From my dreams, I made the decision to stop channeling and clear some things to strengthen my connection.)

J: *Yes, something amazing is about to happen. You needed to clear some of your residual anger for you to handle what is coming. You got the message very quickly, and for that, I am grateful.*

B: What an amazing month I had. I felt you with me many times. I hope you know how grateful I am for your presence, even when I had to disconnect from it all.

J: *Oh, Bruce, you may have stopped channeling, but you were hardly disconnected. Did you ever sit back and notice just how many people came to your aid and how things lined up for you? You truly have many angels, guides, and souls cheering for you and creating your path. You have no idea. Think back to when you had the bio-energy healing. Do you remember the first day when she said that many angels were present? Imagine the largest football stadium you have ever seen, watching and cheering you on at full capacity. That is close to the number of angels and guides who were there at that time.*

B: Oh my, I can't even imagine. Why me?

J: *I wish I could say that you are the only one, but I can't. The angels and ascended masters are all watching many and bringing them together to bring forth a work that I find difficult to explain in earthly terms. This is all part of the flow that I told you about during your third session with the bio-energy healer. I wish I could tell you, but part of this thing called faith requires you and many others like you to learn to trust the flow and learn to live by that trust. It is so important that you just do this. I know that you want answers. I know that you want to know exactly what will happen, but trusting the flow and having faith that the next step will be provided is critical.*

B: I am like a kid at Christmas, I really want to know what is under the tree, but I get the sense that as with any great learning, there needs to be an obstacle and, in some ways, pain, as much as I don't want to admit it. My greatest learnings have been through the adversities that we face on earth.

J: *You are right. There will be much learning to come. The best thing I can tell you is what I told you before: trust the flow. Have you noticed that some of the best things that have happened to you have been a combination of flow and adversity? When things appear to be difficult, always look for the energy current that is constantly moving through all situations. It will always take you to where you need to be.*

B: As you were telling me that, I just saw images of many times in my life where that has been true.

J: *See, you know it already.*

B: (Smiling) Yeah, I guess I do.

Seventh Discussion

B: Today, I had a dream when I took a short 15-minute nap. You were in my dream for the first time in a long time. In the dream, you told me to FaceTime you. I said okay, but then I realized that that is not possible since you do not have an iPhone. I woke up so disappointed. Was that my imagination, or was it you?

J: *What do you think?*

B: I was kind of hoping that it was you.

J: *(Smiling) It was me, but it was more of an astral plane meeting.*

B: Were you joking when you asked me to FaceTime you?

J: *Not really. I had a couple of reasons for telling you that. First, I wanted you to begin the conversation again, but secondly, I wanted to give you an idea of what is to come.*

B: What is to come?

J: *Yes, in the not-too-distant future, if you keep working at raising your vibration, we will be able, at times, to hold face-to-face conversations, much like you can FaceTime with your kids now. Of course, I do not mean new technology, but this is a vibrational thing. The higher the vibration, the more the veil thins. Keep in mind that just like when you have a remote conversation, you cannot experience everything you can in person, but you can have glimpses of a person or people in other dimensions. Many people can do this now through a trance channel, but this is a little different. This process is more like pulling back a curtain. Some on earth can do it now, but it will be for you to learn how.*

For you to do this, every day, you must practice raising your vibrations. How much easier will it be for us to communicate when you can do that.

B: That sounds incredible. What other advice do you have for me?

J: *Finish this book, because there is so much more that you are on earth to do. The earth is changing, it will be a difficult time for many, and you are here to be a bridge.*

B: You are scaring me now.

J: *Oh, my dearest one, I do not mean to do that to you, but you have to understand just how important your life's mission is. I will be with you, as will countless beings from the angelic realm. This is not only important to you but the entire earth. You and many others will be using your spiritual gifts to bring about this change. Many will look to you and those around you to show them the way. What is happening now will be told throughout all eternity as one of the greatest triumphs of the earth's experience. I can tell you this process is not only healing for the human but every creature and the earth itself.*

Don't you want to be part of that story?

B: Well, when you put it that way, I am looking forward to it.

Eighth Discussion

B: Wow! I have felt your presence all day. I love that full-body vibration that I receive when you are present. What is that?

J: *That is my natural vibration. In the future, you will recognize it as my signature, but it will not be so strong as it is now. Because you are at a lower vibration most of the time, you notice it more. I am not saying that it is bad. Earth has so much dense energy, and to function there you have to live at that frequency. That is why it is so important for you to practice raising your vibration. You will feel lighter, and your energy levels will increase.*

Ninth Discussion

(Note: I had a dream and Michael interpreted it on his radio show.)

B: I recently had a dream, and as the dream was interpreted, I learned that I have the gift to rearrange others' karma. This may sound crazy, but I believe that it has something to do with creating a path by which they will more easily fulfill the karmic obligations, as some people's karma can become so overwhelming that it limits their ability to complete their life plan. I had a knowing last night that I first learned of this gift when I was Bundelé and that it had something to do with mitigating your karma, as you were suffering so much from your husband's abuse at the time. Will you speak to that? Did Bundelé do that for Jitara, and how much were you aware of it, if at all?

J: *Oh, yes, it is very true. I make no excuses for my husband's actions other than to say, life was not easy, to begin with. We were poor. I continued to get pregnant, and he blamed that on me. With each child, there was another mouth to feed. I was the person he blamed, and was also the one who would ask for the money to buy food for the family. He did not want to take responsibility for his contributions to the problem and used me to represent everything wrong in his life. Yes, he beat me, sometimes so severely that I would wake in a pool of blood.*

As an escape, I always would try to go to the temple to pray. I would pray not only for my safety but also for my children. Luckily, they were spared from his rage, as he only took it out on me. When I went to the temple, I would take extra caution to cover my wounds and bruises, causing me more shame. I had not provided my husband what he wanted, so he beat me. You really must understand the time period and location that this took place. Still, I do see many women currently that are in the same situation.

When you first asked, I was so ashamed that I had been beaten. Inside I blamed it all on myself. Could I tell you? There was something very soft and loving about you. How could I admit that I was such a terrible woman that my husband had to beat me? I could not bear the thought of you thinking badly of me. I never told you at that time that I had thought about how I could end the pain by ending my life, but thoughts of my children always kept me from that.

Gradually, I gathered my courage, and on one visit, I confessed exactly what was happening. I saw a rage in your eyes that I had never seen before. I was so fearful that you hated me because of the terrible woman that I was. Many feelings of unworthiness, guilt, and self-doubt felt like a sword being thrust into my heart. Quietly and calmly, you told me that all my sufferings were not the direct action of anything that I did, but were part of a cycle of karma. I did not understand. I just knew that I was a bad person who was a terrible wife, but something about your essence was so calming.

I didn't realize it until much after that; it was from that point forward that my husband's attitude towards me began to mellow. I just thought that I was becoming a more acceptable wife, as he was not as angry all the time. Interestingly, as we aged, my husband and I began to reconcile. I can tell you that I overcame the karma associated with that relationship, and the intense pain disappeared.

I never learned what you did until I was part of your life review. I cannot adequately describe the intense feeling of compassion and gratitude that I felt when it was revealed to me. What you may find interesting is that you and my former husband are extremely tight on this side of the veil and have performed similar functions for each other numerous times throughout your souls' journeys.

Tenth Discussion

B: I am getting very close to completing this book. What advice do you have for those who may read this?

J: *Enjoy the ride! I am talking about every beautiful thing and action that you see and the adversities you face. Being human is such a remarkable thing. One day you will look back on it all and begin to comprehend the magnificence in all that you experience and how fortunate you have been.*

Each soul has had hundreds of lives in which they have the opportunity to learn. You are so blessed to have this opportunity. I know that it may be difficult to understand from the human side, but each experience you have on the earth is a blessing. Each morning you should wake with a thankful heart for the opportunity that you have to be there. Do not waste days living in fear, for it is fear that will destroy you.

Chapter 14

What Does it All Mean?

Journey to Oneness

Jessica was originally half of my soul. We are still two parts of a whole. This extends much further than just this "Twin Flame" connection. Each person on earth has male and female energies. Much like Yin and Yang, the object is to keep those energies in balance for optimal health. When they are out of balance, we struggle. This grappling is not necessarily a bad thing, but to needlessly do so does not truly help anyone. For much of my life, I struggled. Looking back, it is clear I was out of balance. Now, I feel a sense of empowerment, and balance, when I am connected to her.

About a month after Jessica came back into my awareness, I had traveled to Vietnam on a business trip. I was there for two weeks, and had a weekend where I could explore. As I considered the places to spend that time, I was drawn back to where I have previously visited. Siem Reap, Cambodia, is home to the world-famous Angkor Wat temple. From the first time that I visited that place, I fell in love with the culture and the people. This time I did not visit the Angkor Wat temple, since I had been there twice before. I instead decided to visit Phnom Kulen National Park.

Phnom Kulen dates back to the ninth century and is a beautiful mix of Hinduism and Buddhism, with both being represented in the same location in harmony. My tour guide that day, Sothea Yon, a former Buddhist monk, brought the spirit of that place alive. A river, Kbal Spean, runs through the area and was the first place we stopped. As we got out of the van, the heat of the Cambodian sun was overwhelming, but as we approached the water I felt a cooling effect.

This river originally provided all the water for the temples in the Angkor Wat area. This river has a nickname, The River of a Thousand Lingas, as in ancient times thousands of lingas were carved into the riverbed. A linga is the masculine interpretation of Shiva, one of the Hindu gods. The riverbed also had areas where a linga was connected to a yoni. The Hindu origins of the yoni indicate it is a feminine representation of the symbol of Shakti, the creative force of the Universe. As Sothea explained, each symbol on its own represents a powerful force, but the union of the two creates a power that moves the Universe.

A month prior, I had learned of Jessica's presence and her importance in my life. I was just beginning to understand what our soul connection meant. Chills ran up my spine and spread through my entire body as I learned that day of the power of the masculine and feminine connection that the symbols in this river represented. I had a soul-level understanding of each symbol's significance, but more than that, it was the understanding of the power of their combination.

A week before Jessica's reappearance in my life, I had had a dream of stepping into and eventually completely immersing myself in a body of water that contained yoni and linga symbols at the bottom. The body of water indicated my spirituality, which was connected to the submerged symbols. In other words, a direct link exists between my spiritual self and the union of the male and female energies. This is true in relationships, but also within each person.

This thing called life is such an interesting thing. It is often so all-encompassing that every decision seems incredibly significant. We live as though our whole existence starts when we emerge from our mother's womb and ends when we return to the womb of mother earth. We become afraid of the little time that we seem to have, but at the same time, we spend most of that perceived brief period living for our future dreams or clinging to the past. Most of us forget about living in the one time that we can control, the present. We sometimes overlook the beauty of mindfully moving our way through life.

What we often overlook is that each of us has experienced hundreds, if not thousands of lives here on this planet. While this life may seem as if this is all we have or ever will know, that is not true. This life is only like putting on a different set of clothing. The only difference is that most of the time, we cannot remember what we wore the last time.

The soul's path is remarkable. The relationships that we form over that journey are infinitely stronger than any one lifetime. We move from lifetime to lifetime, playing various roles, often interacting with the same souls repeatedly. It seems to be a pathway to come to the perfect understanding of Oneness and pure love. Each soul's journey is unique but leads to the same state of being.

Even though I was not allowed to know Jessica in physical form in this life, I am so grateful that she came back into my life when I needed her the most. I cannot begin to express the emotions that I have felt during this journey over the last couple of years. I have experienced pure joy and an intense loneliness such as I have never felt before. And I have learned so much in the process.

Just as one of her friends expressed after she passed, I hope that her face is the first one I see when I die. I am lucky through this journey to have already experienced that moment so many times. I think that it will mean so much more when we are finally permanently together. I can't wait.

Appendix

The First Dream

India (1/6/2018)

[Bruce] I am at a business conference in India. I leave the conference and go around a lake to the other side. It feels like it is the weekend. My hotel is an apartment in a 5-story walk-up. Later, I leave with my father, and we drive to a touristy shopping area that is extremely crowded. I tell my father to wait as I move through the crowded area. I go to the second floor and in a lobby area, I meet my sister. Evidently, that is who I was looking for. As we sit talking, two of her students, to whom she is teaching English, arrive. I have a brief discussion with them to allow them to practice, and they leave with my sister.

[Michael] *India is indeed about karma in this dream. It is backed up by the 5-story walk-up, as five also symbolizes karma. The conference says this dream is about what you planned to do coming here (before incarnating). It's interesting. Your dream actually starts off in the spirit world (the con-*

137

ference), and going around the lake to the other side is about coming to the physical plane. We always hold the stick from the other end, so you must have been asking for a true perspective on your life.

The hotel symbolizes your reception at birth, and the apartment (in a 5-story walk-up) says your karma is to deal with issues around your heart/emotions. Leaving the hotel with your father says you copied your father to a degree. At the very least, you were heavily influenced by him.

So now you have to answer questions about your sister. She can represent herself and/or your female side. The female side fits in well with the apartment symbol. You say that "evidently, that is who I was looking for," so she can indeed symbolize your female side and your search to become aware of that side of yourself.

However, you find her on the second floor - that means you are a channel. I don't know if you're already aware that you have that ability. Your sister has the ability to teach people to communicate. Since channeling is a special communication ability, that too fits with the meaning so far, but really it is not about your sister. It is about your ability, so it is likely that you will teach others to channel. Even in the dream, you help people practice. Your sister is used as the focus of channeling because of something about her. Consider what that is. That's what I meant when I said you have to answer questions about your sister. Note also that your sister has two students on the second floor. The number 2 littered around dreams is common for a channel.

[Bruce] I go back and I find my dad. He is sitting in a wheel-chair at a table with unknown people. He is complaining that because he is in a foreign country, his cell phone will not work. I tell him that we can switch his phone to Wi-Fi mode, and he can connect. Soon, I am outside next to the lake with my dad's cell phone. The water is truly clear, but there is no one in the water, and I am afraid that it may be polluted only because of that.

I accidentally dropped the phone in the water. When I pull it out, it doesn't work. I look beside me, and I notice five large silver rings. They look like championship rings that have been arranged in a row. I wonder what to do with them but then decide to leave them, as someone must have left them there for some sort of good luck or a prayer. As I leave, several of the rings slip into the water.

[Michael] *We can ignore the wheelchair since you said your dad used one. However, it is not your dad at his best. This means influences from your dad hold you back. He's com-plaining in the dream—did he complain a lot in reality? But notice what he is complaining about—difficulty with com-munication (i.e., channeling). Now we also see why it is in a foreign country, too. You've difficulty understanding the communication you receive. Wi-Fi is also about connecting over invisible channels. You've really got channeling showing up in spades here.*

The lake symbolizes an untapped spiritual reservoir. So, you're being pushed to tap into your ability. The water is clear—that's good. Fear of pollution means you're afraid your connection is tainted. I think most people have that concern in the beginning. Dropping the phone in the water is okay in a dream. It shows the connection between the symbols. The phone not working was already the issue. That's what you've to invest in—activating your channeling connection.

A slight shift in the dream here. We still have karma because of the number 5, but the silver rings mean you also have a strong intuitive connection. Hopefully, this is already working for you. It works by getting information like feelings. You should have picked up the five rings in the dream! If you want them, you've to go into the water to get them (just like you did for the phone). That means you've to get into your spiritual nature.

Don't think for a moment that there are people better than you at this (you left the rings for someone else)—it's your karma to develop both your intuition and your channeling ability. I think your channeling will work as thoughts impressed onto your mind. You can discern these from your own thoughts, as they are usually very uplifting. They feel like a solution and never feel like a negative option.

[Bruce] I head back to the apartment, as I want to dry out the phone. I go up and down a 5-floor staircase, but I cannot find the right room. I realized that I am in the wrong bank of stairs. I finally make it to my apartment and begin to dry out the phone. Water keeps pouring from the phone. The more I shake it, the more water comes out. Finally, I get it where some of the lights are starting to return, and so I try to reassemble the phone, but I realize that a small plastic piece is missing. I think that it must have fallen off near the lake. It is starting to get dark, so I hurry back to the lake to look. By the time I get there, it is too dark to find the piece. I reach into my pocket, only to realize that I have had the piece in my pocket the whole time.

[Michael] *Going up and down in this dream is about practicing raising your vibration—i.e., meditation. Realize that it will not immediately bring you to the right place to establish your connection (fix the phone), but it eventually will. So, stick with it.*

Lights starting to return are great. Light is what it is all about. A plastic piece is missing! Not likely. This means you are looking for something man-made (plastic is man-made) to fix your connection. It won't. Not surprisingly, you discover you already have what is needed on you. It is common for channels to have this type of dream when they want a better connection.

[Bruce] I make my way back to the apartment. However, the hallway to get to the apartment is blocked by an old pickup. I squeeze by the pickup, but my camera bag falls off. I look back, and a girl gives me my bag back. She was hiding it. In the apartment, my old boss, Jessica, and my boss' boss, Ted, drop by. I ask them if they need a place to stay for the night, and they tell me that they are not sure but give me a wrapped gift.

[Michael] *The apartment is mentioned again. This is your heart/feelings again. This is where you end up completing the connection. A hallway is a transition. So, you have to overcome your male way of being (old pickup truck) to complete this part of your journey.*

The camera bag seems like it belongs in a different thread, but dreams are never wrong. So there has to be a link between reproduction/sexuality/sexual energy, and you make this connection. Because a girl was hiding it—ask yourself if you are emotionally open (girl hiding it) in this area. The girl gives it back to you, so again your female side is the key.

Being given a wrapped gift is excellent. What are Jessica and Ted's traits? You need to adopt the positive ones that stand out and drop any negatives. These are usually obvious when you think about people. It might only be positive traits too. The gift is what you are after the whole time. The gift of communication with spirits. Indeed, it could also be why your dad is featured in the dream, since he has already passed.

[Bruce] The next day, I, along with the others including Ted, head back to the conference, and we all have our luggage in the back. There is something about my luggage being labeled with "UC" as in UC Berkeley in blue and yellow. As we arrive, I ask the driver if I can leave my bags in the car, as I know that soon we will be leaving for the airport. He tells me no and that it would not be a good idea. I go to the back of the car and pull out my bags. I originally pulled out my traveling companion's bags and thought that I should be nice and take some of them in for her, but I decide that I must let her carry her own.

[Michael] *The luggage here is another symbol for karma. Dealing with your baggage is your karma. Work on yourself to overcome the issues you picked up in childhood from your dad (squeeze past the old pickup truck). It is labeled; UC Berkeley says this is how you will learn about yourself, since*

Berkeley is a university. I just looked up their colors. The yellow is a mustard yellow, and the blue is navy. So, you've to overcome a negative philosophy of life (navy) and let go of irrational fears (mustard yellow). I name the colors just in case they were different in your dream. Anyway, did your dad have these traits, and to what extent did you copy them from him? That's what you've to clear.

Leaving your bags in the car is not a good idea, and the driver is right to refuse. You need to deal with your baggage. Not ignore it. Having to go to the back of the car to pull out your bags shows that your baggage comes from the past (at the back). Pulling out your companion's and almost taking responsibility for them was nearly a disaster. I'm glad you decided to let her carry her own.

So, this is another question. Do you take on other people's responsibilities? If you do, just like in your dream—you need to stop that. They achieve their life purpose by working through their own baggage. Helping someone to avoid that does not help them spiritually. Note: helping people with their karma is okay taking their karma on is not.

Okay, so that's it. The questions I ask are really just rhetorical for you to prompt thought. I know I skipped some symbols, but their interoperation was already covered by others.

Although I say the questions are rhetorical, I'd love to hear your feedback on my analysis.

Current Playlist

Each song has a line or a special meaning sent by Jessica.

Name	Artist
Angels	Robbie Williams
Lay Me Down	Sam Smith
Fall on Me	A Great Big World & Christina Aguilera
Save the Best for Last	Vanessa Williams
A Thousand Years	Christina Perri
Love Me Anyway (feat. Chris Stapleton)	Pɪnk
In Case You Didn't Know	Angelika Vee
In Case You Don't Live Forever	Ben Platt
Un-Break My Heart	Toni Braxton
Look What You've Done to Me	Boz Scaggs
She Knows	Curtis Stigers
I Honestly Love You (1998 Version)	Olivia Newton-John
True Love (feat. Lily Allen)	Pɪnk
Is That Alright?	Lady Gaga
One Day I'll Fly Away	Nicole Kidman
I'll Never Love Again (Extended Version)	Lady Gaga

A Song for You	Donny Hathaway
You	A Great Big World
My Funny Valentine	Curtis Stigers
Home	Foo Fighters
Faithfully	Journey
Lovely Day	Bill Withers
Don't Stop Believin'	Journey
I Need You	Curtis Stigers
Shallow	Lady Gaga & Bradley Cooper
Make You Feel My Love	Adele
Has Anyone Ever Written Anything for You	Stevie Nicks
Just to Be with You Again	Lionel Richie
Your Song	Elton John
Wings (Acoustic)	Birdy
A Million Dreams	P!nk
At Last	Etta James
Something	The Beatles
Never Enough	Kelly Clarkson
Come What May	Nicole Kidman, Cecilia Weston & Ewan McGregor
Sometimes	Alex Slay
Die with You	Eden Mary
The Promise	Tracy Chapman
Calling You	Barbra Streisand

Lesley Ann	David Sanborn
Nature Boy	Nat "King" Cole
I'm in You	Peter Frampton
Just the Way You Are	Billy Joel
Never Saw a Miracle	Curtis Stigers
Hello Again	Ronan Keating
I Still Believe	Claire Moore & Lea Salonga
It Means Beautiful	Dan Gillespie Sells
Valentine (feat. Josh Mortensen)	Evie Clair
The One	Elton John
In This Time	The Tea Party
I Knew This Would Be Love	Imaginary Future
Then Came You	Dionne Warwick
Need You Now	Lady A
I Love You Always Forever (Acoustic)	Mateo Oxley
Inside Your Heaven	Carrie Underwood
Maybe I'm Amazed (Remastered)	Paul McCartney
Climb Every Mountain	Audra McDonald
Play That Song	Train
All I Ask of You	Barbra Streisand

Acknowledgments

Through words, deeds, and pocketbooks, below are the people who helped me along this journey and made this book possible. I am grateful for each one of you in ways you may not imagine.

Scott Dickerson

Randall Jones

Mia Kafkios

Jacki Campbell and Juro Mrsic

Grant and Jamie Haskell

Shelli Shaeffer

Molly Grove

Sheila Delaney Duke

April Angel

Lys Hardy

Cyndy Adams

Asaf Lederman

Camille Ganir

Jami Barney

Brett Hill

Catherine Liggett Moreno

Anne Tucker

Heidi Sheridan

About the Author

Born and raised in Pacific Northwest, Bruce Klein is the father of two remarkable adult daughters and is married to an amazing woman. He spent the bulk of his career in corporate international trade compliance, but before that lived and worked in Asia for over seven years, mostly working in education. During that time, he developed a deep appreciation for the diversity of beliefs represented on that continent.

In 2017, he began to have a spiritual awakening, which led his life down paths that he could not have imagined. This book is the first part of those adventures.

If you would like to contact Bruce, his email address is: **bruce@geminae.net**